*'Abdu'l-Bahá in New York, The City of The Covenant, 1912.*

# 'ABDU'L-BAHÁ IN NEW YORK
# THE CITY OF THE COVENANT

Eliane Lacroix-Hopson

Bahá'í Publications Australia

# 'ABDU'L-BAHÁ IN NEW YORK
# THE CITY OF THE COVENANT

© Eliane Lacroix-Hopson

A First Edition of this book has been published
in New York City, USA. 1999

This Second Edition by
Bahá'í Publications Australia 2005

ISBN 1 876322 32 2

Distributed by
Bahá'í Distribution Services
P.O. Box 300
Bundoora Vic. 3083
Australia
Email address: bds@bahai.org.au

## ACKNOWLEDGEMENTS

A shorter edition of this book has been published in 1987 commemorating the 75th Anniversary of the visit of 'Abdu'l-Bahá to America, and was the collaboration of a group of friends:

Eliane A. Hopson, Research and Writing;
Hussein Ahdieh, Producing;
Juliette Soderberg, Editing;
Al Burley, Photographer;
Hugh Locke, Book Design;
Norma Avegnon, Word Processor;
Mouhebat Sobhani, Contributor.

The 1912 photographs were from the
Estate of Mrs. Asa Cochran,
courtesy of the Hopson/Samuel family.

Published by The Spiritual Assembly
of the Bahá'ís of the City of New York.

Currently:
Feature writer for Yachay Wasip 'Simin' (Voice of Yachay Wasi) a quarterly, published by Yachay Wasi, Inc. (Quechua: House of Learning), a nonprofit Cultural and Educational corp. in New York State and Cuzco, Peru. YACHAY WASI is a Civil Society, NGO United Nations, ECOSOC and DPI.

ALL PUBLICATIONS are entered in the Bahá'í World Centre Library Collection, Haifa, Israel, including a Philosophy of Science book © 1991, unpublished.

# PHOTOGRAPH CREDITS

All 1912 photographs of 'Abdu'l-Bahá are from Mrs. Asa Cochran's estate, courtesy of the Hopson/Samuel family. The picture on p. 54 was taken by renowned Gertrude Käsebier, on June 20, 1912. Translation of 'Abdu'l-Bahá's handwriting inscription:

"O Lord, this handmaiden is working in Thy service, make her victorious."

This comment was addressed to Mrs. Cochran, a New York Bahá'í who had traveled to India for the Faith.

Recent photographs by Michel G. Samuel.

Reprint of 1912 newspaper clippings is from a 1970 collage by Frank B. Sawyer, Sr.

# CONTENTS

FOREWORD ........................................................................................ 9

INTRODUCTION ............................................................................ 13

'ABDU'L-BAHÁ IN THE CITY OF THE COVENANT ................................. 15

THURSDAY, APRIL 11, 1912 ............................................................ 15

THE CHURCH OF THE ASCENSION AND THE
CONTROVERSY THAT FOLLOWED ..................................................... 19

ABDU'L-BAHÁ COUNTERS RACIAL SEGREGATION ............................... 25

THE MASTER RETURNS ..................................................................... 31

THE LAKE MOHONK PEACE CONFERENCE .......................................... 33

ACTIVITIES CONTINUE UNABATED ..................................................... 35

ANOTHER UNIQUE EVENT AT THE CHURCH OF THE ASCENSION ....... 41

THE PAINTING OF 'ABDU'L-BAHÁ'S PORTRAIT ................................... 43

THE BAHÁ'Í ADMINISTRATIVE ORDER AND OTHER LESSONS ............. 45

THE FILMING OF 'ABDU'L-BAHÁ ..................................................... 49

THE CENTER OF THE COVENANT NAMES THE CITY OF
THE COVENANT ............................................................................... 51

THE UNITY FEAST, JUNE 29 ............................................................ 55

NEW YORK CITY'S POTENTIAL ....................................................... 59

'ABDU'L-BAHÁ'S ENCOUNTERS WITH CHILDREN ..................... 63

FULL SCHEDULE OF ACTIVITIES CONTINUES ........................... 65

THE ONENESS OF HUMANITY ................................................... 69

THE FINAL MONTH ..................................................................... 71

THE LAST ORDEAL ..................................................................... 75

THE DAY OF THE COVENANT ................................................... 79

FAREWELL! ................................................................................. 83

IN CONCLUSION ......................................................................... 89

APPENDIX 1 ......................................................................................... 91

TABLETS AND LETTERS .................................................................. 93

THE TABLET OF THE BRANCH ...................................................... 97

TABLETS FROM 'ABDU'L-BAHÁ .................................................... 99

LETTER FROM SHOGHI EFFENDI ................................................. 121

MAJOR ADDRESSES ......................................................................... 123

THE UNITY FEAST ............................................................................ 127

'ABDU'L-BAHA'S FIRST PUBLIC ADDRESS IN
THE UNITED STATES ...................................................................... 127

FIRST ADDRESS ON RACE UNITY ................................................. 131

RELIGION & SCIENCE ...................................................................... 134

THE MOST GREAT PEACE ............................................................... 139

THE EQUALITY OF WOMAN AND MAN ...................................... 143

THE ETERNAL CREATION .............................................................. 148

BAHÁ'U'LLÁH'S EPISTLES TO THE KINGS .................................. 151

TALK ON THE DAY OF DEPARTURE ............................................ 157

APPENDIX 2 ........................................................................................ 161

PLACES 'ABDU'L-BAHÁ VISITED .................................................. 166

SELECTED BIBLIOGRAPHY ............................................................ 169

NOTES ................................................................................................... 171

# 'ABDU'L-BAHÁ'I IN NEW YORK
# THE CITY OF THE COVENANT

## FOREWORD

Priceless eyewitness accounts, written records of 'Abdu'l-Bahá's addresses, and newspapers as well as magazine articles published in a number of volumes constitute a thorough chronicle of the Master's 1912 travels to and through the United States and Canada. The 1987 contribution to the existing body of work was in answer to the wish of the Spiritual Assembly of the City of New York that tablets addressed by 'Abdu'l-Bahá to this community which appeared in a 1932 book entitled *'Abdu'l-Bahá In New York*, long out of print, may be published in observance of the 75th Anniversary of His visit.

Authenticated by Shoghi Effendi's letter reprinted in this 1932 book, these tablets do not appear elsewhere, dates and circumstances surrounding their utterance are not known. They, and the historic events which took place in New York on June 19, 1912, are the basis of New York's distinguished title of "The City of the Covenant."

The meaning of this title is not generally understood. The present book, focusing on the chronology of 'Abdu'l-Bahá's visits in the city and using some material as yet unpublished in this country, attempts to provide a practical frame of reference for study.

The Master did not "tour" the country, He deliberately chose New York as the hub of His travels as He pointed out: "I have always returned to New York, because I wished New York to advance greatly..." Consequently, 'Abdu'l-Bahá's stay in New York City was the longest in one place: 85 days out of 239 in the country. The length of this sojourn and the demanding schedule that He engaged in while in the city are further evidence of the attention the Master bestowed on this community.

9

'Abdu'l-Bahá found the New York of 1912 to be a place of tolerance by comparison with other racially segregated societies and planned the first Bahá'í interracial marriage to take place here. This was an event of great significance at the time, confirming the Master's statement that interracial marriages are "a service to humanity."

New York City welcomed 'Abdu'l-Bahá. Religious congregations, peace societies, and universities vied to invite Him. Bahá'ís and others alike, attracted by His love and wisdom, followed the Master from place to place.

The chronology of the visit of 'Abdu'l-Bahá to New York and the United States is primarily based on two sources: The Diary of Mahmud of Zarkan* and The Diary of Juliet Thompson, from the 1947 version annotated by Miss Thompson.**

Mahmud was one of the Persian secretaries who accompanied 'Abdu'l-Bahá in His travels to the West.

Juliet Thompson, one of the early New York City Bahá'ís, was a renowned portrait painter. Her obituary, published in the New York Times, mentions that she "painted the portrait of President Woodrow Wilson and his Cabinet," among other celebrities. In 1909 Miss Thompson spent two months in 'Abdu'l-Bahá's household in the Holy Land and was privileged to be called by Him "the sister" of His own daughter. In 1911, she was called to meet the Master in Switzerland and she was almost every day at His home in New York.

Juliet Thompson's diary stands out as a phenomenon, unique in the history of religion. In this candid and vibrant testimony, we experience the vicissitudes of a passionate and sincere woman's spiritual experience. Juliet as a painter and a writer brings to life in perceptive details the scenes surrounding 'Abdu'l-Bahá and succeeds in making us feel the reality of the extraordinary spiritual power of One Whom Bahá'u'lláh hailed as "The Mystery of God."

Additional information is from Portals to Freedom, a memoir written by Howard Colby Ives. Reverend Ives was a Unitarian minister from New Jersey who had heard of the Bahá'í Faith at a time of spiritual searching. He had approached 'Abdu'l-Bahá on the first day of His arrival and was with Him as often as he could be, frequently following Him in His travels. He became a Bahá'í before the end of the Master's sojourn in the United States and dedicated the rest of his life to service to the Faith. Portals to Freedom is a recollection of Howard Colby Ives' traumatic experience with the Master, written in 1936 when he was ailing and almost blind.

Other sources are listed in the footnotes and in the Selected Bibliography.

This Second Edition includes added Major Addresses and some corrections.

---

\*   Typescript copy, Archives of the Spiritual Assembly of the Bahá'ís of the City of New York.
\*\*  From the estate of Mr. and Mrs. Edward Kinney, courtesy of Mr. and Mrs. Donald Kinney.

# INTRODUCTION

'Abdu'l-Bahá was the eldest Son of Bahá'u'lláh, the Prophet Founder of the Bahá'í Faith. His claimed station was the "Servant of Bahá," a Servant of His Father's Cause, a divine revelation from God which initiated a new age in the evolution of humankind.

Bahá'u'lláh designated 'Abdu'l-Bahá "The Center of His Covenant" and called Him "The Master," a title which was also respectfully used by the followers of the Faith in the United States when referring to 'Abdu'l-Bahá.

Bahá'u'lláh and His family were dispossessed of their ancestral properties and exiled from Persia in 1853, when 'Abdu'l-Bahá was a child nine years old. They remained prisoners of the Ottoman Empire in Akka (Akko or Acre, in today Israel) until the Young Turks' Rebellion of 1908 freed 'Abdu'l-Bahá and His family from prison.

After a period of rest, 'Abdu'l-Bahá decided to travel to the West to spread the message of Bahá'u'lláh. The Western Bahá'ís had been pleading with the Master to visit America.

An American Bahá'í, visiting 'Abdu'l-Bahá in Palestine wrote excitedly to a friend in August 29, 1910: "I have a very big piece of news to tell you. 'Abdu'l-Bahá has left this Holy Spot for the first time in forty-two years and has gone to Egypt." The day of His departure He had visited the pilgrims (other visitors) as usual; they did not suspect that it was a good-bye visit.[1]

In 1911, 'Abdu'l-Bahá made His first historic trip to Europe, then He returned to Egypt, in Ramleh, a suburb of Alexandria, until the spring of 1912. On March 25, the Master and His retinue boarded the S.S. Cedric in Alexandria, heading for the United States. The American Bahá'ís had sent thousands of dollars for His journey, urging Him to leave the Cedric in Italy and travel to England to sail on the maiden voyage of the Titanic. But the Master returned the money for charity and continued His voyage on the Cedric.

'Abdu'l-Bahá's entourage was an unusual mixture of Easterners and Westerners. The Master usually wore a long robe, white or light tan, a dark aba (overcoat) and a white turbaned headdress on His flowing, silky white hair. The Persians in His entourage wore Western clothing and the red fez. At Naples, a few Americans and an English believer, Miss Louisa Mathew, joined the traveling party for the rest of the trip.

At the table, "the intermingling and assembling together of the Easterners and the Westerners attracted the eyes," wrote Mahmud. It also caused misunderstanding and distrust due to the war between Turkey and Italy at the time. However, during the voyage, the officers of the ship asked 'Abdu'l-Bahá to address a public meeting which they arranged in the lounge. Among the large number of people attending were the consuls of Russia and Italy, who conversed regularly with the Master afterwards.[2]

Twenty five years later, a woman who as a child had traveled on the Cedric told a Bahá'í that she had never forgotten her personal encounter with the Master. "A glance that burned" into her soul and frightened her, lest she had displeased Him, and the kindly smile which released her "from terror." She recalled that everyone had remarked about "His majestic bearing, His kingly walk, and above all the strange white light that followed Him everywhere." [3]

# 'ABDU'L-BAHÁ IN THE CITY OF THE COVENANT

## 'ABDU'L-BAHÁ'S ARRIVAL, THURSDAY, APRIL 11, 1912

The momentous arrival of 'Abdu'l-Bahá in New York City occurred on the morning of April 11, 1912. On the tugboat that met the ship bringing 'Abdu'l-Bahá and His entourage to this country were newspaper reporters, among them Wendell Phillips Dodge of the New York City News Association. Mr. Dodge gives an account of the appearance and remarks of the Master:

"His face was light itself... He is a man of medium height, though at first sight he seemed to be taller... As he paced the deck, talking to reporters, he appeared alert and active in every movement, his head thrown back and splendidly poised upon his broad shoulders most of the time... When the ship was abreast the Statue of Liberty, standing erect and facing it, 'Abdu'l-Bahá held his arms wide apart in salutation and said, 'There is the New World's symbol of liberty and freedom. After being forty years a prisoner, I can tell you freedom is not a matter of place. It is a condition... When one is released from the prison of self, that is indeed a release.'... Going up the river, gazing in a look of bewildered amazement... at the downtown skyscrapers, the "Wise Man out of the East" remarked: 'There are the minarets of the Western world's commerce and industry.'

Dodge stated: " 'Abdu'l-Bahá comes on a mission of international peace, to attend the Peace Conference at Lake Mohonk and to address various peace meetings, educational societies, religious organizations, etc..."

Wendell Phillips Dodge's lengthy article was distributed around the world by the Associated Press and more than a dozen other newspaper accounts appeared in and around the city.[4]

*The Ansonia, Broadway and 73rd Street, where 'Abdul'l-Bahá stayed during His first nine days in New York. The Master occupied a 2-bedroom, 1 drawing room suite on the 7th floor. This building is now designated as a landmark and is a condominium.*

By the time the S.S. Cedric docked, a crowd of Bahá'ís had been waiting for hours, eager to meet 'Abdu'l-Bahá. However, one of the American believers, Mr. Edward Kinney* was called forth to board the ship, and he returned with a message from the Master that He would meet the friends at the home of Mr. Kinney at four o'clock.

'Abdu'l-Bahá and His entourage were driven from the ship to the Hotel Ansonia, Broadway and 73rd Street, His headquarters for the next nine days of incredibly intense activities. After resting and having a cup of tea, He was taken to the home of Mr. and Mrs. Edward B. Kinney, where hundreds of Bahá'ís had gathered. "Almost everyone was weeping just at the sight of Him." The Master addressed a warm welcome to all, then had a few words with each one.[5]

'Abdu'l-Bahá spoke a little English and it was often apparent that He understood it well. He addressed his audiences in the Persian language (Farsi), each sentence followed by a translation. His retinue of Persian friends were learned translators and secretaries. People commented that the translation did not seem necessary at times as they felt the meaning of His words through the power of "His flashing eyes," His gestures and His warm, smiling countenance.

The next day, April 12, set the pattern for all His days - that of a continuous flow of activities. In the mornings, people streamed in line at the Ansonia to meet Him, each one receiving a measure of His love. As recalled by Reverend Howard Colby Ives, the experience was dramatic: "Life has never been quite the same since."

In the afternoon, 'Abdu'l-Bahá traveled to Brooklyn, to the home of Mr. and Mrs. Howard MacNutt, where He addressed an audience in the hundreds. Back in Manhattan in the evening He spoke to hundreds of people in the studio of Miss Phillips. "The enormous room was packed," confirmed Juliet.[6]

The following morning, as all mornings to come, was spent with an endless flow of visitors. Among the clergymen present was Reverend J.T. Bixby, a Unitarian minister who was writing an article on the Bahá'í Faith for the North American Review.

Rev. Bixby is described as self-important and verbose to the embarrassment of everyone present. At last, 'Abdu'l-Bahá led him to the door and laughing, took a large bunch of red roses and laid them in the arms of the surprised visitor, now humbly bowing, to everyone's mirth.

During the afternoon of this April 13, 'Abdu'l-Bahá addressed a large assembled group at the elegant home of Mr. and Mrs. Alexander and Marjorie Morten, celebrated patrons of the arts. The Master spoke of "the Season of Creation and the evolution of the Spiritual Springtime" when the translator experienced a blank... dead silence... 'Abdu'l-Bahá, laughing, supplied the missing word: "Summer!" A ripple of delight went through the sophisticated audience which was captured by this moment of warm humanity.

---

\* Mr. and Mrs. Edward and Carrie Kinney, their two children, Juliet Thompson and a friend had been on an eight month pilgrimage in Akka in 1909 and had offered their home to the Master. "They spared neither time nor effort or money to have everything as well arranged for 'Abdu'l-Bahá as possible during His sojourn in New York City." Shoghi Effendi called Mr. and Mrs. Kinney "Pillars of the Faith in the City of the Covenant" and "Pillars of the Cause of God." Bahá'í World XII, pp. 678-9; XIII, p.865.

# THE CHURCH OF THE ASCENSION AND THE CONTROVERSY THAT FOLLOWED

The visit of 'Abdu'l-Bahá on Sunday, April 14, to the Church of the Ascension, Fifth Avenue and 10th Street, was an historic day of triumph for the Bahá'ís of New York City, and particularly for Juliet Thompson who was a parishioner of the church. The Church Rector, Dr. Percy Stickney Grant, a personal friend of Juliet, had been persistently hostile toward 'Abdu'l-Bahá and the Faith, but in a change of mind had offered his church for the first official appearance of the Master in New York. 'Abdu'l-Bahá accepted the offer above thirteen similar invitations.

Dr. Grant was a brilliant but opinionated Christian clergyman who, during 'Abdu'l-Bahá's sojourn, was torn between conflicting allegiances. He was touched by the Master's love and majesty, and deeply moved by the momentous sense of history conveyed by His personality and mission. For 'Abdu'l-Bahá's visit he had spared neither publicity nor preparation. He had reached "perfection," wrote Juliet, in the decoration and organization of the service: the summit of pomp and circumstance.

Dr. Grant opened the service with the reading of prophecies pointing to Bahá'u'lláh and of the 13th Chapter of Corinthians, instead of the traditional lesson for the day. 'Abdu'l- Bahá was waiting in the vestry. Then, in the thunder of organ music and the triumphant singing of "Jesus Lives," the Master entered the chancel in a kingly manner, Dr. Grant holding His hand, leading Him to the Bishop's Chair. In front of a throng of two thousand, Dr. Grant introduced with the greatest respect and emotion the One he had previously fiercely denounced from his pulpit. He spoke from the chancel, then stepped aside as 'Abdu'l-Bahá replaced him in the same honored place.

*Church of the Ascension, 5th Avenue and 10th Street, where 'Abdul'l-Bahá gave His first public address, April 14th, 1912.*

We can imagine this unforgettable scene for those Bahá'ís present: 'Abdu'l-Bahá standing in His white, flowing robes, surrounded by a lavish profusion of lights and calla lilies, His turbaned head haloed by the rays of the sun filtering through the colored windows, dominating all with simple, majestic dignity, His arms outstretched.

His vibrating, melodious voice started: "In his scriptural lesson this morning the revered Doctor read a verse from the Epistle of St. Paul to the Corinthians, 'For now we see through a glass darkly, but then face to face.' The light of truth has heretofore been seen dimly through variegated glasses, but now the splendors of divinity shall be visible through the translucent mirrors of pure hearts and spirits." And the Master went on to extol the mission of Jesus and Bahá'u'lláh, establishing a divine civilization and world peace.

When He ended His address, 'Abdu'l-Bahá was asked by Dr. Grant to give the benediction. His face uplifted, His eyes closed, the palms of His hands in offering to God, 'Abdu'l-Bahá chanted a prayer, the clergymen kneeling on each side of Him.

"... Too great to put into words, it was almost too great to bear..." wrote Juliet in exaltation. She was probably echoing the feelings of the Bahá'í friends on that day. After the service, the Master went to His car, while the neighborhood resounded with cries of "Alláh'u'Abhá" from the believers. Mr. Grant's mother, a friend of the Bahá'ís, ran to the Master, crying for joy at His knees.

In the afternoon, 'Abdu'l-Bahá spoke at the Union Meeting of Advanced Thought Center at the Carnegie Lyceum (now Carnegie Hall.)

The following day witnessed a controversy, the result of the Master having been seated in the Bishop's Chair in the Church of the Ascension and addressing the congregation from the chancel: An Episcopalian Canon had been broken! Newspapers took sides and were not quieted until the Bishop himself went to the Ansonia to visit 'Abdu'l-Bahá and thanked Him for honoring the Church with His visit. The Master replied with talk of "the injuriousness of dogmas and imitations."

*Pencil portrait of 'Abdul'l-Bahá by Kahlil Gibran, April 15th, 1912.*

To Dr. Grant, He sent the message, "Say: I will not forget the services thou hast rendered yesterday. They are engraved in the book of My heart. Thousands of years hence, the mention of yesterday will be heard and it will become history that you were the founder of this work. I will never forget the love which was manifested yesterday." [7]

It was on the same day, April 15, according to the biographers of the renowned and celebrated Lebanese poet and painter, Kahlil Gibran, that a beautiful pencil portrait of 'Abdu'l-Bahá was drawn by Mr. Gibran. This portrait was done as part of a series of drawings of well known personalities and artists most respected by Gibran, including Auguste Rodin and Claude Debussy, among others. The series appeared in major exhibits in New York and Paris, and was acclaimed to be the best work of Gibran, who acknowledged drawing to be his favorite medium.

In "Juliet Remembers Gibran," the Bahá'í writer Marzieh Gail, recalls a 1943 conversation with Juliet about Kahlil Gibran, who lived in a studio across the street from her home. They were close friends, and Gibran loved 'Abdu'l-Bahá. He was inspired to write "Jesus, the Son of Man" from his recollection of the Master. Gibran had asked Juliet to request the Master to sit for him. He was accorded one hour at 6:30 in the morning. Gibran's biographers place this event on April 15, the day of the sinking of the Titanic.* Writer Barbara Young, in "The Man from Lebanon," mentions that this event took place in the studio of the artist. However, it is likely that at this early hour it was in the Master's suite at the Ansonia Hotel. [8]

News of the sinking of the luxury liner, the Titanic, on her maiden voyage, was announced in the newspapers April 16. After praying for the deceased, the friends offered thanks that 'Abdu'l-Bahá had not traveled on that ship. This day was filled with the usual flow of morning visitors, a public meeting in the afternoon at the home of Mr. and Mrs. Arthur Dodge, and in the evening, the Master addressed friends who had come from New Jersey to visit Him at the Ansonia.

Commenting to Mr. MacNutt upon the newspaper accounts of the sinking of the Titanic, 'Abdu'l-Bahá reflected on the fact that material achievements of technology and wealth are in vain unless man builds a spiritual civilization in his own heart. "... I wish you to live in the world of the Spirit... beyond the gloomy mask of this mortal existence..." After a long pause, the Master said: "I was asked to sail upon the Titanic, but my heart did not prompt Me to do so."**

\*     "Kahlil Gibran: His Life and World". K. Gibran had moved from Boston to New York as a protégé of arts patrons Marjorie and Alexander Morten, identified as Bahá'ís and active pacifists. A dozen references describe their activities in this book, more particularly on pp. 273, 387-8. The portrait of the Master is reproduced on p.288.

**     Star of the West, Vol.3, p.210.

# ABDU'L-BAHÁ COUNTERS RACIAL SEGREGATION

'Abdu'l-Bahá deplored the racial segregation prevalent in the United States and He "strongly urged the friends to associate with each other in the utmost joy and happiness." He called for such a gathering, and it took place Wednesday, April 17, at the home of Mr. and Mrs. Kinney, where Bahá'ís and their friends of both the black and white races met in unity. He prepared and served the meal Himself, speaking of the human family as "a garden of flowers of various hues." The Master was most happy and the spirit of the friends was high. It was felt that this was a landmark in the city. This memorable event was followed by a public address at the hotel.

While pouring out love to everyone, expounding on the Teachings of the Faith, and traveling from place to place in the city, 'Abdu'l-Bahá's humaneness was always apparent. He often showed His emotions, He laughed, He wept. During a talk at the home of Mr. and Mrs. Marshall L. Emery, He was so anguished in His recollection of the sufferings of Bahá'u'lláh that the entire audience was moved to tears.[9]

Friday, April 19 was a very busy day for the Master and the friends.

In the early afternoon, 'Abdu'l-Bahá had been invited to attend a play at the Little Theater, "The Terrible Meek," depicting the Crucifixion of Christ, and the Master said to have wept along with the audience.

At 5 pm, at Earl Hall, Columbia University, professors, scholars, students and others heard Him speak on "religion, science and universal peace." He was invited to visit the various departments of the University, but He had to decline for lack of time. This was followed by a return to the Ansonia, where He was met, as usual, by

*Entrance to Columbia University Earl Hall where 'Abdul'l-Bahá gave "His" "Religion and Science" talk on April 19th, 1912. Note the appropriate dedication over the door. "Erected for the students that religion and learning may go hand in hand and character grow with knowledge."*

a crowd of waiting people. Among them was Kate Carew, a reporter for The New York Tribune.

We have an excellent description of 'Abdu'l-Bahá in a feature article Miss Carew wrote in which she depicted Him as being of "scarcely medium height, but so extraordinary in the dignity of his majestic carriage that he seemed of more than average height." She appeared not only totally bewildered by the diversity of the crowd but also impressed by the personality of the Master and His warm response to each visitor. 'Abdu'l-Bahá invited Miss Carew to accompany Him and a few others to His next engagement at the Bowery.

The unusual and moving event at the Bowery Mission was the confirmation of several weeks of Juliet's teaching and dedication. She had spoken about the Faith and the life of 'Abdu'l-Bahá to the derelicts, and in turn, they invited the Master to speak to them. 'Abdu'l-Bahá had previously given $500 to Juliet and to Mr. Edward Getsinger for them to change into two large bags of silver quarters. After a loving talk to about 400 men, the Master stood at the door waiting for them to file by. He looked ahead appraising each man, then pressed some coins into his hand. One of them, John Good, a former criminal who had reformed since Juliet befriended him, declared that the Master had justly appraised each man's need and had given accordingly.

Returning to the hotel by taxi, the Master was amused by the glittering of Broadway's electric signs, and was reminded that Bahá'u'lláh loved light, recommending that His household economize on everything except light.

At the Ansonia, the Master emptied the remaining coins into a maid's apron, who, upon learning of the Bowery event, promised that she would also give this money to the poor. She wanted to say goodbye to 'Abdu'l-Bahá, crying that she had been blessed to serve him, and asked for prayers.

The Master had invited the friends for a late supper in His suite. Recalling the performance of "The Terrible Meek" which He had attended early in the day, He said the play depicting the Crucifixion

*The Bowery Mission, where 'Abdul'l-Bahá delivered an address to an audience of 400 poor people, placing coins in the hand of each man as he left the meeting. The Bowery Mission is still a haven for the downtrodden as seen in this photograph.*

of Christ, should have been more complete. The Master then, told of the life and suffering of Jesus, in so detailed and vivid terms, that He seemed to relive events of "remembered anguish." He also commented on the power of the theater which could influence human feelings in reviving an event which took place 2000 years ago.

Of the mornings at the hotel, Juliet Thompson wrote: "Oh, those mornings at the Ansonia in the Master's white sunny rooms, filled with spring flowers and roses! People poured in to see Him in droves, sometimes a hundred and fifty in one morning! Exhausted, He received the late arrivals in bed... I would watch them go into His bedroom and come out changed, as though they had had a bath of Life." Charles Rand Kennedy, author of "The Terrible Meek," was there one morning, and deeply moved said: "I was in the presence of God."[10]

On April 20, 'Abdu'l-Bahá left for Washington as the first stop of a three-week tour of Bahá'í communities. In Washington, journalists wrote that 'Abdu'l-Bahá swept through the Capitol, the Supreme Court, and the Congress "saw fit to adjourn."

A number of Washington Bahá'ís belonged to the highest strata of society. Receptions organized for 'Abdu'l-Bahá included the elite of government, diplomatic and academic circles. The Master addressed a large interracial gathering at Howard University and expressed happiness, but He sternly commented to His entourage about the evidence of racial prejudice He had witnessed. He related that He had ordered interracial meetings. "The attendance was very large, the colored people predominating. At our second gathering this was reversed, but at the third meeting, We were unable to say which color predominated. These meetings were a great practical lesson upon the unity of colors and races in the Bahá'í Teachings." [11]

*This new church replaces Grace Methodist Church destroyed by fire and where on May 12th 1912, 'Abdul'l-Bahá addressed the International Peace Forum.*

# THE MASTER RETURNS

Saturday, May 11, returning from a trip which included, on May 1st, the official laying of the cornerstone of the Bahá'í House of Worship in Wilmette, Illinois, 'Abdu'l-Bahá moved to a top floor apartment in the Hudson Apartment House. To those joyously gathered around Him, He said: "It is only three weeks that we have been away from the New York friends, yet so great has been the longing to see you that it seems three months." [11]

On Sunday, though still tired, 'Abdu'l-Bahá went to the Unity Church in Montclair, New Jersey. The minister, Dr. Edgard Wiers, had invited the Master and now introduced Him with great respect and emotion "as One of the Great Prophets, Chosen Ones of God."

'Abdu'l-Bahá spoke on the Oneness of God and Creation, and ended chanting a prayer. A deeply moved audience followed Him to the street, all eyes brimming with tears of joy. After an afternoon shared with a group of friends, the Master returned to New York to address the International Peace Forum at the Grace Methodist Church. This was another triumph as the large attendance gave a standing ovation at the end of a major talk on the Bahá'í Teachings and history, and the establishment of the Most Great Peace.

On May 13th, 'Abdu'l-Bahá was to appear as the guest of honor at a meeting of the New York Peace Society held at the Hotel Astor. The Master was sick in bed with a high temperature, Juliet pleaded for Him to rest. "I work by the confirmation of the Holy Spirit. I do not work by hygienic laws. If I did, I would get nothing done," He laughed.

The peace meeting was an impressive gathering of two thousand people. On the dais was a group of leading personalities of the time: Rabbi Stephen Wise, president; Mr. Short (a friend of philanthropist Andrew Carnegie); Mrs. A. G. Spencer of the Ethical Society; Dr. Percy Grant; Professor William Jackson of Columbia

University, and Mr. Topakyan, Persian Consul General. They all made introductory remarks. Mr. Topakyan said: "Our guest of honor has stood as a Prophet of enlightenment and peace for the Persian Empire, and a well-wisher of Persia may well honor Him... In closing, I am happy to say that 'Abdu'l-Bahá is the Glory of Persia today." This was not the only laudatory remark; they all vied to express their reverent admiration, recognizing the spiritual leadership of this "Great Figure from the East."

Though the Master was visibly tired and His voice was hoarse, He delivered a unique speech on the Teachings of Bahá'u'lláh for the age and on the establishment of peace.

"There is no doubt that... the banner of international agreement will be unfurled here to spread onward and outward among all the nations of the world."* The response of the audience was such that Mahmud was ecstatic: "Verily, no desire remained unfulfilled to us, the servants of the Covenant. We saw with our own eyes the victory and confirmation of the Kingdom of Abhá." After the meeting, the audience pressed to come near to the Master, "He shook hands with... everyone of those two thousand people!" wrote Juliet.

Later, back at the Hudson Apartments, a group of Japanese and Indian people were waiting for Him. The Master welcomed them and spoke on the civilization of India and the divine civilization.[12]

*Hotel Astor, location of The New York Peace Society's meeting where 'Abdul'l-Bahá was the guest of honor on May 13th, 1912. This then fashionable hotel on Time Square has been demolished. (From New York State Bahá'í Bulletin, 1977)*

---

* "The Promulgation of Universal Peace" p. 125.

# THE LAKE MOHONK PEACE CONFERENCE

Juliet Thompson had previously introduced the Faith to Mr. Khan Bahadur Alláh-Bakhsh, the Governor of Lahore. On the morning of May 14th, this gentleman came to meet 'Abdu'l-Bahá who, warmly, welcomed him. The Governor sent a letter to Juliet stating: "'Abdu'l-Bahá is the Divine Light of today."

On the same day, the Master traveled to Lake Mohonk, New York, for three days at the National Conference on Peace and International Arbitration.

In 1911, 'Abdu'l-Bahá had exchanged correspondence with Mr. Albert Smiley, Founder and President of the Conference. As a result, He had been invited to be the featured speaker at the 18th Annual Conference and the Master had scheduled His visit to the United States to include this important event.

These Conferences were attended by prominent people of New York, Washington DC, and other cities and countries. 'Abdu'l-Bahá spoke on the first day on "The Oneness of the Reality of Humankind." Many in attendance were impressed and came on the platform to thank Him, some embracing Him with emotion.

The Master also gave two general addresses on the teachings of the Faith and many private talks. His main address and commentaries were featured in the Conference report and two of His speeches were published in New York newspapers.

On the last evening, 'Abdu'l-Bahá had expressed regrets that He should have brought a Persian rug as a gift for Mr. Smiley. Dr. Zia Bagdadi took the challenge of going to the New York apartment to fetch the rug during the night, and to be back in time before the planned departure. After an epic trip by various cars and trains, Dr. Bagdadi arrived in the mailman's horse wagon when the Master was leaving, shaking hands with Mr. Smiley. Receiving the rug, this gentleman exclaimed that this rug was similar to one destroyed in a fire and his wife, still heart broken over the loss, will be very happy.[13]

Although 'Abdu'l-Bahá greatly enjoyed the beautiful scenery, and the comfortable and quiet setting of Lake Mohonk, He was glad to come back to New York. He loved the Riverside Park area. He had selected a secluded spot there where He liked to go daily and walk by Himself or "sleep on the grass" a few minutes to rest. "When I am alone, exhaustion is removed and I am relaxed," He said. Sometimes, He allowed the friends to go with Him to this "hallowed spot," "His Garden," as the friends named the place and a recurring name in Juliet's and Mahmud's diaries.

*"The Garden of 'Abdul' l-Bahá". Riverside Drive Park area across West 78th Street where the Master resided looks very much as He loved it in 1912.*

# ACTIVITIES CONTINUE UNABATED

On Sunday, May 19, 'Abdu'l-Bahá spoke at the Church of the Divine Paternity on Central Park West. The church's Byzantine architecture seemed a natural frame for the Master who was often referred to as "the Patriarch of the East" because of His Eastern robes and headdress. The people attending were touched by the beauty of the scene as well as captivated by 'Abdu'l-Bahá's address on progressive revelation and the Teachings of Bahá'u'lláh. Miss Thompson was astonished to see a man she knew as a staunch atheist who looked as captivated as the rest of the audience. This person went regularly to visit the Master at His home afterward.

In the afternoon, 'Abdu'l-Bahá went to Jersey City to speak at the Brotherhood Church where Dr. Howard Colby Ives was the unsalaried Pastor. Reverend Ives ended his introduction with these words: "My friends, the Kingdom of God is at hand, and I call upon you to recognize it! I call upon you to spread the news on every side!"

On Monday, at a Woman's Suffrage meeting at the Metropolitan Temple, the Master's topic was education and the rights of women. He brought in stories about some of the great women in history, including Mary Magdalene. A flow of emotion stirred some of the audience to tears.[14]

The following day, Tuesday, May 21, "the fashionable world," including artists and writers, met 'Abdu'l-Bahá at a reception given in His honor by Mrs.Tatum, a devoted Bahá'í and a socialite. In His address to the large group, He spoke of His years in prison and the contrast of being there in this friendly home, associating with such personalities. "Think of it. Two Kings* were dethroned in order that I might be freed. This is naught but pure destiny, and now, you here in America must work with me for the peace of the world and the oneness of mankind."

*Church of the Divine Paternity, Central Park West and 79th St. where 'Abdu'l-Bahá spoke on May 19, 1912.*

Dr. Percy Grant was in the audience and the following day said to Mr. MacNutt: "As I listened, I realized profoundly that this was an historic moment; that before me sat One Who, imprisoned for the sake of humankind, had been freed by the Power of God alone through the dethroning of two kings." Dr. Grant then extended an invitation for the Master to come back to the Church of the Ascension, to the People's Forum on June 2.[15]

'Abdu'l-Bahá spent four days in Boston, then, returned to New York on May 26. After a brief rest at the home of the Kinneys, although still very tired, He proceeded to Mount Morris Baptist Church (now Mount Moriah) where He was scheduled to address the congregation. Juliet Thompson wrote: "This church suggests an old synagogue and the Master looked Christ-like to the friends." This spiritual feeling is described by Mahmud: "'Abdu'l-Bahá was standing under the arch of the church and reclining exhausted against the pillar... That night all saw with their outward eyes the effect of the Holy Ghost. Let no one think that it is only word painting. Yes, the tongues and feelings of all present bear a testimony to it. I write this because it is my duty to record it... all the non-Bahá'ís looked upon the Beauty of the Covenant as a Prophet."

As the landlord at the Hudson Apartments complained about the excessive number of visitors and that his staff could not cope with the extra labor and problems, the Master decided to rent a house. In the meantime, He stayed for a few days at the Kinney's home, then moved at the end of May to a house owned by Mr. Champney, 309 West 78th Street.[16]

'Abdu'l-Bahá received a continuing flow of invitations from churches, educational organizations and other groups. In the evening of May 28, He was the main speaker at a peace forum held at the Metropolitan Temple. This was a major reception attended by leading personalities and more than a thousand people. The Master was introduced as "the representative of the International Peace Movement... promoting the unity of all nations as the need of this age..." Author Frederick Lynch made the welcoming address. He said to have followed the Master to several places, and expressed his feelings with emotion: "In Mohonk, 'Abdu'l-Bahá gave the most remarkable address, expressing the highest principles of His teachings... How I welcome this great man whose presence has inspired and attracted the minds of Americans. He receives inspiration from the breaths of the Holy Spirit. His spirit is infinite, unlimited and eternal. I am happy ... to be given the opportunity to express publicly my innermost testimony."

The Master spoke on the Oneness of God and unity of His Prophets as the source of the oneness of mankind and peace. Rabbi Silverman, previously hostile to the Faith, was visibly moved and responded to 'Abdu'l-Bahá's words with high praise: "We have seen today the light with our own eyes... The spiritual lights have always shone from the East upon the West. The world is in need of these lights... The fountainhead of these lights has today spoken before

*The Hudson Apartment House, 227 Riverside Drive. 'Abdul' l-Bahá top floor residence from May 11th to May 26th, 1912, when the landlord complained about "the excessive number of visitors" his staff could not handle.*

38

us... His love and teachings have captivated the hearts of the Americans." "This change of mind is the greatest proof of the majesty and the power of the Covenant of God," commented Mahmud.

Two evenings later, 'Abdu'l-Bahá addressed an audience at the Theosophical Lodge on the evolution of the spirit through the realms of creation. Also He spoke at New York University on science and divine philosophy.[17]

On Friday, May 31, the Master was welcomed by friends in Fanwood, New Jersey, where He gave talks at two places and at the Town Hall. He returned to New York the following day and met with the large number of people, both friends and seekers who were, as usual, waiting for Him.

* Sultan 'Abdu'l-Hamid of Turkey and Shah Musaffarid-Din of Persia.

# ANOTHER UNIQUE EVENT AT THE
# CHURCH OF THE ASCENSION

On the evening of Sunday, June 2, as previously invited by Dr. Grant, 'Abdu'l-Bahá was the guest speaker at a People's Forum at the Church of the Ascension. These meetings were less formal and the participants were invited to ask questions.

The Master gave a powerful talk on the requested topic: "What can the Orient bring to the Occident?" Juliet recalled that the previous year, Dr. Grant had preached on the same topic in negative terms toward the Faith. Now beautiful words were praising Christ and the Law of God, represented by the firmness of Peter and the Church as a collective center for humanity. In our time, this same collective center, it was pointed out, is the revelation of Bahá'u'lláh and a civilization of peace.

Dr. Grant, visibly shaken, praised the Master and fielded questions from the large audience while 'Abdu'l-Bahá responded warmly. Seated at the center of the chancel, He enjoyed the exchange. At ease, "He pushed back His turban and smiled as He answered, often very wittily."

Mahmud marveled at witnessing the respectful audience, the sight of which "no written words can describe." Afterward, the Master confided that arriving at the church, He hadn't felt well enough to speak, "... but when I stood before this gathering I found the atmosphere of the church full of the Holy Spirit and a state of wonderful happiness and joy came upon Me." [18]

On going to the Master's home the next morning, Juliet found Him in the street near "His Garden," with a group of friends whom He was anointing with attar of rose. Then He welcomed a young man who turned out to be Walter Hampden, the actor playing the part of Jesus in a play. Mr. Hampden, afterward, came every day to visit.

Later on that day, upon having been invited, 'Abdu'l- Bahá traveled to the estate of an unidentified U.S. Cabinet member, where He spent the night. A social gathering was held, attended by notables and national statesmen, who were respectfully attentive to the Master's utterances. One gentleman inquired about the possibility of international war. 'Abdu'l-Bahá spoke of this event as likely: "Great ravages will take place in Europe. Great empires will crumble and will become petty states."

The following day, before leaving the estate, the Master called the servants, and thanking them distributed a gift of money to each one of them. Back home, He found the many friends waiting for Him and spoke at length to them.

The Master's whirlwind activities continued and the fifth of June saw Him in Brooklyn. He first attended a children's affair sponsored by the Union League Club of Brooklyn. A luncheon was served for civic leaders and guests which included Admiral Peary, the explorer of the North Pole as featured speaker. He had met 'Abdu'l-Bahá in Washington and expressing his admiration for Him, requested a talk. The Master spoke on education. Then, in the evening, He went and spoke at a meeting of the Women's Union.

On June 8, although exhausted, 'Abdu'l-Bahá went to Philadelphia at the invitation of several churches. He came back to New York two days later, refreshed by the love of the friends and the enthusiastic response of the congregations He had visited in Pennsylvania.[19]

# THE PAINTING OF
# 'ABDU'L-BAHA'S PORTRAIT

'Abdu'l-Bahá had expressed a desire for Juliet to paint His portrait and He requested that she come to His home on June 1st, at 7:30 in the morning, to begin work on it. She was given three sittings: the first one on that day, the final two about two weeks later.

"I went into a panic," she confessed. The light and the location in the basement were poor, and "how could I paint the Face of God?" "I want you," He said, "to paint my servitude to God." "Oh, my Lord," she cried "only the Holy Spirit could paint Your servitude to God... Pray for me!" "I will pray," answered the Master, "and as you are doing this only for the sake of God, you will be inspired." "And then, an amazing thing happened. All fear went away from me... I painted in ecstasy, free as I have never been before." [20]

*Juliet Thompson's pastel painting of 'Abdul'l-Bahá. From a 1912 Ms. Thompson's photograph. The original painting taken by the Master to the Holy Land has been lost.*

# THE BAHÁ'Í ADMINISTRATIVE ORDER
## AND OTHER LESSONS

On June 11, after morning prayers and tea, 'Abdu'l-Bahá spoke to the assembled friends about the role of the future House of Justice which will ensure the continuity of the Faith. Later that day, He gave two talks at His home and received the usual stream of visitors. Juliet noticed how tired He looked, still talking to all: "It was pure sacrifice!"

That very night at the home of the Kinneys, there was a Board of Council* meeting. The Master came and "striding up and down like a king, He explained the meaning of Bahá'í Assemblies to the friends, inspiring them to become "telegraphic stations... one of the wires attached to the souls, the other fixed on the Supreme Concourse."

During the next two days, June 12 and 13, Juliet went early in the morning to the beloved house to work on her painting. The flow of visitors made it a bewildering experience: "So wonderful... so humanly difficult... from room to room, one kind of light to another." She had one sitting on the 13th, and actually this was the third half-hour promised by the Master. Each time the "miraculous thing" happened and she worked "in rapture." The painting was practically finished, afterward whenever she tried to go back for more detail something always seemed to interfere.

On the 14th, Juliet arrived early hoping to work, but 'Abdu'l-Bahá had left already. She stayed with one of the Persian friends who recalled memories of his father. Valiyú'lláh Khán was the son of Varqa Khán, a Bahá'í Martyr and renowned poet, very dear to Bahá'u'lláh. Varqa Khán had told his son that Bahá'u'lláh had explained to him the Station of the Master as "The Mystery of God," a Station although not of a "Manifestation of God" (a Divine Prophet), was of the same spiritual nature and power for a certain purpose in the Plan of God.

Varqa wrote poems to the Glory of the Master, Who would scold him for it. Varqa could not keep quiet and wrote:

"O Dawning-Point of the Beauty of God,
I know Thee!
Though Thou shroudest Thyself in a thousand veils,
I know Thee!" **

Besides receiving daily morning visitors and friends, some with petitions, 'Abdu'l-Bahá wrote tablets in answer to His voluminous mail. Though He would escape as much as He could to "His Garden," and He tried to limit individual requests for interviews to urgent matters, the Master found the daily process exhausting. Yet He did not cease speaking to the friends in groups on various aspects of "this Great Dispensation."

On the afternoon of June 15, 'Abdu'l-Bahá came down to the waiting crowd of friends. He told them that while resting, He had dreamt that he was speaking to them at the top of His voice. The sound of His own voice awakened Him with the word "distinction." He explained the meaning of distinction in every kingdom of Creation. "I desire distinction for you. The Bahá'ís must be distinguished from others ... but not of any worldly distinction. For you, I desire spiritual distinction." [21]

On June 16, 'Abdu'l-Bahá was invited to speak at the Fourth Unitarian Church, in Brooklyn, and the Pastor had posted on the church's outdoor signboard:

"The Great Persian Prophet, His Holiness 'Abdu'l-Bahá, will speak in this church at 11am on the 16th of June."

The Persian friends were amazed that a Christian church would recognize the Master as a "Prophet." The Pastor came to greet 'Abdu'l-Bahá at the door and led Him to the pulpit where He spoke.

At the end of the service, the congregation pressed around Him. The Minister asked the Master to speak to the children of Sunday School. They flocked to Him in earnest, and He called them "beautiful children of the Kingdom." The prayer He revealed for them remains a favorite to this day: "O God... These children are the

46

plants of Thine orchard, the flowers of Thy meadow, the roses of Thy garden..."

Lunch was served at Mr. and Mrs. Howard MacNutt's home. That evening, at a meeting at the Central Congregational Church on Hancock Street in Brooklyn, 'Abdu'l-Bahá gave one of His major addresses, speaking with the power of majesty on progressive revelation, with emphasis on Muhammad, and the station of Bahá'u'lláh and His proclamation to the kings and rulers of His time. The Pastor was so transported that he pleaded with 'Abdu'l-Bahá for another visit.

The next day, the newspaper The Brooklyn Eagle published the complete transcript of 'Abdu'l-Bahá's address with a description of the gathering.

The following morning, speaking of His day in Brooklyn, the Master said: "I established the Truth of Islam in the great churches in this day. What have the Moslems now to say to us?" Later, He encouraged the friends to visit the sick, and to travel to teach the Faith in foreign countries.[22]

---

\*   These "Boards of Council" were precursors of today's Local Spiritual Assemblies.

\*\*  J. Thompson's Diary, pp. 309-10

*Still from the film of 'Abdul'l-Bahá shot at the MacNutt home on June 18th, 1912. 'Abdul'l-Bahá with Lua Getsinger, right, and Mrs. MacNutt, left.*

# THE FILMING OF 'ABDU'L-BAHÁ

During His stay at the Ansonia, a commercial movie company had requested to make a short film of 'Abdu'l-Bahá for its newsreels. The Master replied at once, "Khaili Khub" (Very good). Some of the friends were upset and explained to Him that this film would be scattered around the country and used in movie houses. He replied: "Besyar Khub" (Most good!)

Consequently, one day, He appeared at the entrance of the Ansonia for the making of a short film. "It was a wonderfully impressive sight, for as He approached the camera, he was exhorting Bahá'u'lláh to bless this means for the spreading of the Heavenly Cause throughout the world."

The friends arranged for a longer film to be made at the home of Mr. and Mrs. MacNutt on June 18, and they also made a recording of 'Abdu'l-Bahá's voice chanting "Glad tidings! Glad Tidings!"

"Rejoice! Rejoice! The Sun of Reality has dawned!
"Rejoice! Rejoice! The New Jerusalem has descended from Heaven!
"Rejoice! Rejoice! The Glory of Carmel has shone on the worlds!"

Although unskilled handling of the camera had 'Abdu'l-Bahá going out of frame and back again, this is a precious legacy, the record of the Beloved Master in action. The film and recording have been duplicated and sent out to all countries where Bahá'ís resided at the time.

Seventy years later, the film has been incorporated into "The Quiet Revolution," a 58 minutes major film on the Bahá'í Faith, a 1985 BBC production released on English national television and in New York City in January 1986.

At the end of this memorable day, 'Abdu'l-Bahá traveled 40 miles to visit a Jewish friend who was sick, returning home at night utterly exhausted.[23]

# THE CENTER OF THE COVENANT NAMES
# THE CITY OF THE COVENANT

June 19th was an historic day for the Bahá'ís of New York. On that day, 'Abdu'l-Bahá named their city the "City of the Covenant." Also, He spoke of the Tablet of the Branch* revealed by Bahá'u'lláh in Andrianople, and proclaimed His own station as the "Center of the Covenant." 24

What a highly dramatic, almost terrifying moment in history! The Son of Bahá'u'lláh, the Prophet of God for our time, suddenly lifting the veil of His humanity, appearing in the Glory of the Power of the Covenant, the Power of Creation! It happened with the swiftness and blinding energy of a bolt of lightning, transporting its two witnesses, Juliet Thompson and Lua Getsinger,** into a spiritual whirling of exaltation and fright.

Juliet had been called to work on His portrait on that day. She describes a sense of "peculiar power... in the Master's steps while coming down from His room... a fearful majesty... strange flashing of the eyes..." evoking an Old Testament Figure. Later as He was sitting for His portrait, Juliet recalled the following events:

"I had just begun to work, Lua in the room sitting on a couch nearby, when the Master smiled at me, then turning to Lua said in Persian: "This makes me sleepy. What shall I do?"

"Tell the Master, Lua, that if He would like to take a nap, I can work while He sleeps."

But I found that I could not. What I saw then was too sacred, too formidable. He sat still as a statue, His eyes closed, infinite peace on that chiseled face, a God-like calm and grandeur in His erect head. Suddenly, with a great flash like lightning He opened His eyes, and the room seemed to rock like a ship in a storm with the power released. The Master was blazing! "The veils of glory," "the thousand veils" had shriveled away

51

in the Flame and we were exposed to the Glory Itself! Lua
and I sat shaking and sobbing. Then He spoke to Lua. I caught
the words, "Munádíy-i 'Ahd" (Herald of the Covenant).
Lua started forward, her hand to her breast. "Man?" (I?), she
exclaimed. "Call one of the Persians. You must understand
this."
Never shall I forget that moment, the flashing eyes of 'Abdu'l-
Bahá, the reverberations of His Voice, the Power that still
rocked the room. God of lightning and  thunder! I thought.
"I appoint you, Lua, the Herald of the Covenant. And I AM
THE COVENANT, appointed by Bahá'u'lláh. And no one
can refute His Word. This is the Testament of Bahá'u'lláh.
You will find it in the Holy Book of Aqdas. Go forth and
proclaim,
    "This is THE COVENANT OF GOD in your midst."
A great joy had lifted Lua up. Her eyes were full of light. She
looked like a winged angel. "Oh, recreate me," she cried,
"that I may do this work for Thee!"
By now I was sobbing uncontrollably.
"Don't cry, Juliet," He said. "This is no time for tears. Through
tears you cannot see to paint."
I tried hard to hold back my tears and to work, but painting
that day was at an end for me. The Master smiled lovingly.
"Juliet is one of my favorites because she speaks the truth.
See how I love the truth, Juliet. You spoke one word of truth
to me and see how I have praised it!"
I looked up to smile in answer and in gratitude, then I was
overwhelmed again by that awful convulsive sobbing. At this
the Master began to laugh and, as He laughed and laughed,
the strangest thing happened. It was as if at each outburst He
wrapped himself in more veils, so that now He looked
completely human, without a trace left of His superhuman
majesty. Never had I seen Him like this before and I never did
afterward."
(At one time, 'Abdu'l-Bahá had explained that "laughter is
spiritual relaxation." Now the Master very tenderly endeavored to

52

make Lua and Juliet laugh.)

"Perhaps He had just found it necessary, after that mighty Declaration, to bring us down to earth again. He had revealed to us "The Apex of Immortality." He had lifted us to a height from which we could see it. Now He, our loving Shepherd, had carried us in His own arms back to our little valley and put us where we belonged."

In the afternoon of that day, He sent Lua down to the waiting people to "proclaim the Covenant," then a little later, He followed her and spoke on the Station of the Center of the Covenant, "but not as He had done to Lua and me." [25]

In confirmation of His explanations, the Master had the Tablet of the Branch read to the friends so they could hear these mighty words of Bahá'u'lláh:

"Whosoever turns to Him hath surely turned to God and whosoever turneth away from Him hath turned away from my Beauty, denied my Proof and is of those who transgress." [26]

On that same day a copy of the book, "The Brilliant Proof," written by Mírzá 'Abu'l Fadl was received. It was in answer to Reverend P. Easton's virulent criticism of the Faith in London and his letter to America, warning people of 'Abdu'l-Bahá's dangerous influence. The Master was very pleased with the book and ordered its translation to be published in this country.[27]

This Mighty Day ended like an ordinary day, with more visitors requesting an interview.

---

\* In the Bahá'í Writings, Bahá'u'lláh referred to Himself as a Tree, (The Tree of Life, His children as "Branches" and "Leaves".'Abdu'l-Bahá is entitled "The Greatest Branch.

\*\* Lua Getsinger was one of the first Bahá'í pilgrims to Akka in 1898. 'Abdu'l-Bahá had chosen her for her passionate and irresistible nature to be a "Banner" and inspired her to teach "day and night." Though sick, until her death in Cairo 18 years later at the age of 45, she never spared herself and was given the title of "Mother-teacher of the American Bahá'í Community" by Shoghi Effendi, besides the title of "Herald of the Covenant" given by the Master. *Bahá'í News*, April 1976.

*Portrait of 'Abdul'l-Bahá by renowned Gertrude Käsebier, taken June 20th, 1912. Written inscription by the Master is addressed to Mrs. Asa Cochran who had traveled for the Faith.*

54

# THE UNITY FEAST, JUNE 29

On June 20, 'Abdu'l-Bahá agreed to a photographic session at the renowned Gertrude Käsebier's Studio. He approved and chose the proofs He liked.

While preparing for His departure the next day for a ten-day visit to Montclair, New Jersey, the Master announced to the friends that they would be joining Him there for a "Unity Feast," and they would be His guests.

In New Jersey, He stayed at a rented house, going to the market every day and preparing the meals Himself for invited friends and visitors. In general during His travels, He would always supervise kitchen matters. For Himself, He required the least possible amount of food, but for His guests He provided lavishly.

Until June 29, when the Unity Feast was to take place, 'Abdu'l-Bahá spoke at various places every afternoon and every evening. On the 29th, He went to the home of Mr. Roy Wilhelm, in Englewood, for the Feast. On this day, the friends came from New York and the neighboring area.

The grounds of Mr. Wilhelm's home were beautified by a pine grove, surrounded by lawns spread with flowers of every hue, and tables had been set up under the trees.

Seated on an armchair in the shade, the Master looked rested and loving. The friends surrounded Him on the lawns. He greeted every newcomer and asked two ladies to sit on either side of Him-Mrs. Krug, young and elegant, and a very old lady in shabby clothes. They both had the same radiant look, their love for the Master shining like a fire in their eyes raised toward Him.

He spoke to the friends: "This is a delightful gathering... This is a New Day and this hour is a New Hour... Such gatherings as this, have no equal or likeness in the world of mankind... This assembly

*'Abdul'l-Bahá and part of the attendance at the Unity Feast on June 29th, at Mr. Roy Wilhelm's home, Englewood, New Jersey.*

has a name and a significance which will last forever. Hundreds of thousands of meetings shall be held to commemorate this occasion and the very words I speak to you today shall be repeated in them for ages to come..."*

At the end of the talk the meal was ready, but a sudden storm blew up and big drops of rain splashed on the tables. The Master walked calmly in His ivory and white flowing robes, went out toward the road, took a chair which had been stranded there and sat down, His head toward the sky. The Persian friends who had followed Him were behind the chair. After a while, a strong rushing wind raced the dark clouds away and the sun shone again. The Master rose and returned to the grove, smiling at the children who rushed toward Him.

Lovingly, He went among the 250 guests with a vial of attar of rose, anointing each one of the friends while a Persian meal was served. Then He went into the house to meet with visiting ministers. After dark, some 60 people were lingering, unable to tear themselves away from this place of love, unity and beauty. The Master talked to them by the light of candles held by the ladies seated on the lawn: "It was a resounding call to arise from the tomb of self in this Day of the Great Resurrection and to unite around Him to vivify the world." He left them, disappearing into the night: "Peace be with you. I will pray for you." His melodious voice chanted the last words echoing forever in their hearts.[28]

On the following day, 'Abdu'l-Bahá was the guest of Mr. Topakyan, the Persian Consul General in Morristown. The reception was attended by prominent people and members of the press. At night, the Master returned to New York.

---

*     This event is commemorated every year at the same location, on the last Saturday of June.

*Hotel Plaza visited by 'Abdul'l-Bahá in July 1912.*

# NEW YORK CITY'S POTENTIAL

'Abdu'l-Bahá once said: "I desire to make manifest among the friends in America a new light, that they may become a new people, that a new foundation may be established and complete harmony realized, for the foundation of the Faith of Bahá'u'lláh is love." And one evening, answering the Persian friends' question, the Master confided that He was staying a long time in New York because "it is the meeting place of the East and the West. I desire to make it a Center of Signs. I stay here so the friends may advance in spirituality and gain precedence." This was an endless task for the Master in these days.

'Abdu'l-Bahá knew of New York City's potential for greatness. He was heartened by the love and vitality of the Bahá'í community but saddened by the display of lavish luxury. As He was invited to the Hotel Plaza, He chose to sit in one of the smallest rooms of the hotel. He told the Persian friends that whenever He encountered magnificent buildings He was reminded of the dark pit of Tihrán, the desolate barracks of Akka and of the sufferings of Bahá'u'lláh.*

A major article on 'Abdu'l-Bahá and His teachings appeared in Hearst's Magazine. The Master commented that all activities and the response of the people and the press were "confirmation ... through Bahá'u'lláh's Bounty and Favor... We are like flutes and all these tunes are from Him."

Mahmud wrote of the many newspapers articles in praise of the Master. The best were sent to the friends in Eastern countries to share with them, for them to realize how much Western society was impressed by 'Abdu'l-Bahá's teachings and the inroads made by Bahá'í concepts in the minds of the people. Everywhere, poems and songs were written by many in honor of Him and His Faith.[29]

*Side entrance of the American Museum of Natural History on 79th Street, 'Abdu'l-Bahá went through on July 8th, 1912 for His visit to the Museum.*

The Mayor of New York, Honorable William S. Gaynor, had invited 'Abdu'l-Bahá to be with him, on July 4, on the parade reviewing stand. As this was not a religious event, the Master sent Persian friends to represent Him. They were respectfully welcomed and, in spite of the hot weather, Mahmud was quite impressed by the attention given them and by the pageantry of the event.

In the evening, the Master lovingly prepared a reception for Mrs. Thompson's (Juliet's mother) birthday at His home.

During one of 'Abdu'l-Bahá's morning walks in His Garden, a group of people of Greek ancestry passing by were attracted to Him and began to ask questions. The Master talked to them about Greek philosophy and history. They were so captivated that they came back in the evening to join the Bahá'í friends and became frequent visitors afterward. One of the Greek seekers invited 'Abdu'l-Bahá to meet more of his friends in a park outside Manhattan. They went by subway and the Master mentioned that He preferred traveling by surface railway.[30]

Juliet relates that on July 8th, 'Abdu'l-Bahá expressed the desire to visit the American Museum of Natural History. The Master laughed at the size of a huge whale, saying that "...he could hold seventy Jonahs!" He was very interested by the Mexican exhibit, pointing out the relationship of glyphs with Persian and Egyptian art. Answering a question, He assured that in the distant past the continents of Asia and America had been connected before a great catastrophe.**

This was a very hot day, 'Abdu'l-Bahá appeared very tired and sat on the grass outside the Museum as if waiting for someone. An old watchman came, the Master welcomed him warmly and started to explain to him, in simple terms, the relationship of the spiritual world to the material one: "When in a house you go upstairs, the lower floor is still under you." The old man looked startled, then his whole face lighted up: "I see!"

A few days later Juliet, thinking that she should have invited the old man, went back to the Museum and inquired about him. No one knew of any old watchman... She wondered why 'Abdu'l-Bahá wanted to visit a Museum of Natural History under the sun on a blistering July day? Had He instead, knowingly, visited a soul whose dread of death retained him to the lower floor?

\*     From H.M. Balyuzi "'Abdu'l-Bahá." P.226
\*\*    Hopi ancestral tradition relates a similar story and a similar theory is currently accepted by scientists. In many of His Writings and in some of His talks in Europe and America, 'Abdu'l- Bahá often referred to scientific knowledge and concepts well ahead of His time, such as the feasibility of space travels. (Paris Talks, 1913)

# 'ABDU'L-BAHÁ'S ENCOUNTERS
# WITH CHILDREN

One evening Juliet and some of her friends were following 'Abdu'l-Bahá down the paths of His Garden when a band of screaming children rushed out from the bushes, laughing and throwing stones at the group. The Master swept at them at a distance, saying with sorrow: "The people of the world are blind." The children "melted back into the shadow as if they had never existed." Later the Master added, "they laughed at Me, yet My dress is the dress of Jesus, just the same that He wore."

On the very next day, Juliet and a friend followed 'Abdu'l-Bahá's party going to visit Mr. and Mrs. Harris in a tenement neighborhood. There was another group of children who almost spontaneously left their games and followed the Master like "a children crusade." Juliet was struck by the contrast with the strange incident the previous night. A little girl asked her: "Please, Ma'am, is He Christ?" While talking to the children, Juliet sent her friend to inform the Master, now at the Harris' home, of the incident. She came back with the Master's invitation for the children to join Him the following Sunday at the home of Mr. and Mrs. Kinney.

Howard Colby Ives described a lovely scene he witnessed that Sunday at the Kinneys' home, which by now he was visiting on a regular basis. On this day, looking out the window, Reverend Ives was astonished to see a group of some thirty "noisy, not too well dressed... urchins, but spruce and clean, enter the house." He followed them upstairs where 'Abdu'l-Bahá greeted them, one by one, with smiles and laughter. The last one was a dark colored boy and when the Master saw him, His face lit up with a heavenly smile, and He exclaimed: "Here is a black rose!" Everyone present was impressed with a feeling of wonder, which increased when 'Abdu'l-Bahá, distributing a handful of chocolates to each child with a kind word, picked up a particularly dark chocolate and "without a word, but with a humorously piercing glance that swept the group, laid the chocolate against the black cheek. 'Abdu'l-Bahá's face was radiant... and that radiance seems to fill the room." The children looked with real wonder at the colored boy as if they had never seen him before. "As for the boy, himself... his eyes fastened with an adoring, blissful look upon the Master... For the moment he was transformed. The reality of his being had been brought to the surface and the angel he really was revealed." [31]

# FULL SCHEDULE OF ACTIVITIES CONTINUES

'Abdu'l-Bahá's activities from the middle of July until July 23rd, when He left for a sojourn in New Hampshire, included a morning visit to the home of Juliet Thompson where Kahlil Gibran had a private meeting with Him, and where He met some of the friends in Juliet's studio on the fourth floor. On that same day, Mahmud noted that 'Abdu'l-Bahá had met with Reverend Grant and that he was visiting Him "frequently showing great humility and reverence." In the evening, at His home, the Master gave a talk to a large audience.

"This was the day of victory," proclaims Mahmud on July 14th as a multitude waited for the Master at the All Souls Unitarian Church. 'Abdu'l-Bahá delivered a major address on the teachings of Bahá'u'lláh and in conclusion chanted a prayer. "A new spirit was engendered in every heart... Though the Master was discomforted by the hot weather, He stood on the dais while the people filed by to shake His hand with great humility."

The evening found 'Abdu'l-Bahá in New Jersey at the home of Roy Wilhelm in West Englewood, where a group of seekers had declared their faith in Bahá'u'lláh.[32]

The hectic schedule and the sweltering weather were taking their toll. The Master was very tired, and on the 16th of July He went to Brooklyn to enjoy a relaxing time at the home of Mr. and Mrs. MacNutt. The following day he returned home, radiant from the renewed energy found in the love of the Brooklyn friends.

To a lady doctor inquiring about the causes of calamities and troubles in the world of Creation, the Master explained that there were two kinds of calamities. Some are the consequences of man's misconduct and ignorances; others are the results of the exigencies of the contingent world and the unfoldment of the divine law, such as changes, life and death, and are inevitable. As all events are

65

*48 West 10th Street: Juliet Thompson's rented house as it stands today, in the celebrated landmark area of Greenwich Village. A new owner remodeled the house covering up Ms Thompson's studio skylight. The 1912 vine which climbed up to the roof of the 7-storey building next door, has been uprooted long ago as a nuisance.*

interrelated, increased ills and calamities may ensue from man's actions.*

In the evening 'Abdu'l-Bahá was very happy as He chanted a prayer at the wedding of Harlan Ober and Grace Robarts, and He witnessed the marriage vows according to the laws of Bahá'u'lláh. The Master had asked Reverend Ives to perform the legal ceremony since Bahá'í marriage was not recognized at the time.[33]

Juliet attended the wedding, going along with her colored maid who wished 'Abdu'l-Bahá would bless her little boy. After the ceremony, Juliet took the child to the Master Who simply, sat him on His knees, talking playfully with him. Little George was so impressed that back home he told the story excitedly to his step-father, and asked: "Is this the same Master that holds the moon in His hand and makes the sun shine?" **

On Sunday, July 21st, 'Abdu'l-Bahá had been invited by the Consul General of Turkey to a reception at his home. The Master was introduced by Mr. Topakyan, the Consul General of Persia, to a distinguished audience of dignitaries. In the evening the Master met with a group of Armenians.

The next day, 'Abdu'l-Bahá had the joy of receiving the visit of a Bahá'í friend from France, the distinguished Orientalist Hippolyte Dreyfus.*** Later, He had a lengthy meeting with Prince Muhammad-Ali Pasha, brother of the Khedive of Egypt. When back in Egypt, the Prince published an account of his travels, referring to his encounter with 'Abdu'l-Bahá in admiring terms.

In 1929, Martha Root, a renowned Bahá'í traveler, visited Prince Muhammad-Ali in his palace in Cairo. The Prince spoke at length of 'Abdu'l-Bahá as he recalled how proud he was to witness the high station and prestige of the Master in New York. He said "I loved and admired 'Abdu'l-Bahá, and I felt that He loved me as a good friend."****

Among the magazine articles then published, a Harper's major story on Bahá'u'lláh and 'Abdu'l-Bahá concluded in these words: "They live their religion as well as teach it. This is their power."

'Abdu'l-Bahá left on the morning of July 23 for New Hampshire and an historic sojourn at Green Acre, where Sarah Farmer and her father had established a center for educational exchange which was frequented by educators and scholars of international reputation, as well as spiritualists. The Master's appearance had a great impact. Later Miss Farmer willed the school and all her properties to the Faith. Green Acre is today the best known of Bahá'í educational institutions.[34]

---

\*  Again, this concept is now a scientific theory known as "the flight of the butterfly" explaining the interrelatedness of events. It is also part of other advanced theories.

\*\*  A 1947 footnote in Juliet's Diary recalls that in 1925 a handsome young man visited her. This was George, who came to tell her how the Master's blessing "had lived like a fountain in his heart" in spite of his sufferings along with his people. He had a vivid recollection of the Master's appearance at Juliet's home, when he had thought he was seeing God. During the second World War, Juliet heard of George again: He was a medical doctor caring for the wounded in a London hospital.

\*\*\*  Professor Dreyfus was the first French Bahá'í. He translated several books of Bahá'u'lláh's Writings which were published by the Presses Universitaires de France in 1902, and are reprinted to this day. Mr. Dreyfus married distinguished Bahá'í Laura Barney, translator of "Some Answered Questions", a transcript of 'Abdu'l-Bahá's answers to the questions she asked during one of her visits to Akka.

\*\*\*\*  The Bahá'í World, Vol. IV, p.431.

# THE ONENESS OF HUMANITY

While in Dublin, New Hampshire, 'Abdu'l-Bahá announced the forthcoming marriage of Mr. Louis Gregory, a Washington lawyer of black heritage, with Miss Louisa Mathew of London, a white lady. The wedding was planned for the 27th of September in New York City. Though the Master was in Denver, Colorado, on His way to California on that day, this union was His work and the ceremony was performed in the City of the Covenant, as He had expressly wished. The simple ceremony at a Church of England took place with nine persons present, including the minister and his wife, a friend of Jewish background, and representatives of the Bahá'í Spiritual Assemblies of New York, Philadelphia and Washington.[35]

For years, a number of Bahá'í communities had been torn by misunderstanding over racial unity and the concept of interracial marriage implied in the teachings of Bahá'u'lláh. 'Abdu'l-Bahá had invited an unsuspecting Miss Mathew to travel with Him on the Cedric to America, and during the voyage had gradually prepared her to understand His wishes. She had met Mr. Gregory the previous year in Egypt in the presence of the Master. They were both middle-aged, mature persons who respected and were fond of each other. They understood the desire of 'Abdu'l-Bahá to make an example of their union as a service to the Faith, and their profound love for the Master gave them the courage to confront the social prejudices prevalent at the time. Their marriage was a happy one, and 'Abdu'l-Bahá described it as "an introduction to the accomplishment of good fellowship between black and white." [36]

*Mr. Champney's house, 309 West 78th Street, rented by 'Abdul'l-Bahá until the end of His sojourn. Mr. Champney owned these twin houses of similar architecture. The Master's house, right, has been partly destroyed by fire. Intact are the entrance and the first room, right, where 'Abdul'l-Bahá proclaimed His station as Center of the Covenant of Baha'u'lláh, on June 19th, 1912.*

# THE FINAL MONTH

'Abdu'l-Bahá returned to New York on November 11, after a journey of about three months and three weeks, which had taken Him north to the Montreal area in Canada, across the United States, back and forth, including twenty-five days in California. Fortunately, Mr. Champney's lovely house, so dear to the friends, was available for renting again. Mr. Champney and his relatives had become Bahá'ís by this time.

This was the last month of 'Abdu'l-Bahá's sojourn in America; 23 days remained before His departure, and His task was not yet done. In 1912, very few of the Bahá'í Writings had been translated into English; consequently, Bahá'ís at the time had little concrete basis to rely upon in the deepening of their Faith. One major accomplishment of the Master's lengthy visit was the many opportunities He had to present the Bahá'í teachings with thorough explanations to various audiences. These utterances were trustfully recorded and carbon copies of the transcripts were already circulating among the friends.

As timely as the Bahá'í teachings were to the needs of mankind, Bahá'ís in those days lacked the perspective of history to appraise the true dimensions of the Faith, the unique phenomenon which the Bahá'í Revelation constitutes in the spiritual and social evolution of mankind and which is implied in the concept of "the Covenant of God."

To insure the integrity of His Mission, Bahá'u'lláh had designated 'Abdu'l-Bahá as the Center of His Covenant, the sole Interpreter of His Revelation. From the start of His ministry, 'Abdu'l-Bahá had been confronted by opponents justly known as "Covenant breakers." In 1912, some of these misguided and confused individuals lived in Chicago and were disrupting the unity of the Bahá'ís. The concept of "unity" being inherent to the fundamental structure of the Bahá'í Faith, more was at stake in Covenant-breaking than the creation of a splinter group or sect.

The primary purpose of 'Abdu'l-Bahá's journey to America was to officially proclaim His Station as the Center of the Covenant, to rally the unity of the Bahá'í Community, and to establish the strong foundation of love and integrity upon which the future of the Faith of Bahá'u'lláh would stand and progress.

With complete disregard for His frail physical condition, the Master gave most of His time in America to the friends, to their spiritual needs, to turn their weaknesses into springboards for future greatness, to weave a web of love connections between them. Answering their ceaseless inquiries, He patiently nurtured each one of them into the Faith. As Reverend Ives noted, "He sought the soul, the reality of everyone He met." Much was accomplished in this direction, particularly in New York City. On July 16, Mahmud could observe: "His extended stay in New York brought wonderful results among the friends."

On June 19, 'Abdu'l-Bahá had made the official Proclamation of His Station, as "The Center of the Covenant." On that day, the Mystery of God revealed a glimpse of the awesome spiritual power implied in the statement of Bahá'u'lláh:

"Whosoever turns to Him hath surely turned unto God..."

During the three weeks ahead, the last act of this historic drama was to be unfolded. 'Abdu'l-Bahá declined most official invitations and spent the rest of His sojourn perfecting His task of unity. He poured the infinite spiritual power of His divine love into the creative energy which will make the City of the Covenant the "Center of Signs" for centuries to come.

The pattern of these final days was that 'Abdu'l-Bahá spent mornings at His home, then would go to the home of Carrie and Edward Kinney, followed by other visits. He gave only a few public talks. At intervals, He would escape to His Garden to relax and catch the November sun, still bright and warm in New York.

November 12th: The Birthday of Bahá'u'lláh. Some of the friends met at the home of Mrs. Krug who had weekly women's meetings on Tuesdays. Juliet describes the Master's invoking "Ya Bahá'u'l-Abhá" with such force that "... it was as though He were calling Someone on the same plane with Him... and Who would certainly come" and she felt His presence!

Later, 'Abdu'l-Bahá took Juliet to His Garden and instructed her in detail on how to be firm in the Covenant and help bring unity among the friends. "... You must love Me," He said, "for the sake of God." "You are all I shall ever know of God," she cried. "I am the Servant of God," He replied.

Shaken, on the way home Juliet was wondering "Could it be that I was not firm?" The following day, Juliet went early to 'Abdu'l-Bahá's house to thank Him for His mercy and patience with her. "I was asleep and You woke me." The Master replied: "I pray that you may ever be awake. There are a few souls in America whom I have chosen to be teachers of this Cause... I wish you to have all the qualities of the teacher." [37]

Addressing a large number of Bahá'ís at the home of Mr. and Mrs. Kinney, the Master exhorted them "... to strive for the emancipation of their souls from passion and desire... to be aware of selfish ones who would lead them astray from the Path of God." At first, the Master was seated between the two large rooms. Then, He rose in a majestic and dignified manner, His beautiful face transfigured by a powerful emotion and invoking the sufferings and sacrifices of Bahá'u'lláh and the Martyrs, He spoke of firmness in the Covenant. The friends, their eyes brimming with tears, were galvanized.

On the evening of November 15, 'Abdu'l-Bahá was annoyed that some people would comment that they did not see the difference between Christianity and the Bahá'í Faith, or they did not understand the advent of this New Dispensation. En route to the house of Juliet, the Master said: "The time has come for Me to throw bombs!" To a crowd occupying the entire length of the house, He spoke powerfully on the greatness of this Cycle, the great Victories of Bahá'u'lláh over

the Kings and Rulers of His time, and on the meaning of the Bahá'í
Revelation for mankind.[38]

Public appearances during this period included a talk at the
Genealogical Hall, on the evolution of all forms of existence, of
mankind and civilizations. "He ended this address with the chanting
of a prayer which drowned the hearts in a surging sea of ecstasy and
rapture..." commented Mahmud.

# THE LAST ORDEAL

On November 18, upon being invited, 'Abdu'l-Bahá visited the J. Pierpont Morgan Library, where He wrote a few sentences in the guest book, praising the philanthropist and asking God's blessings on his work. The event was reported in The New York Times, including the complete translation of the Master's remark which Dr. Farid had written in the guest book.[39]

In the afternoon, the home of Mr. and Mrs. Kinney became the stage of a drama. "The Master put Howard MacNutt through a severe ordeal, an inevitable ordeal...," commented Juliet.

'Abdu'l-Bahá had instructed Mr. MacNutt with the mission of going to Chicago to meet with the misguided individuals and clarify their status in the Faith. Mr. MacNutt failed to understand the danger of the forces of disunity at this time in the history of the Faith and had avoided the issue, trying to justify his action in a letter to a Persian friend. The result was a dark shadow cast over the community, which since his return was shaken by arguments and uncertainty. Now, Mr. MacNutt was to meet the Master.

In the little time left before His departure, 'Abdu'l-Bahá had to act swiftly. He called Mr. MacNutt in His room, on the second floor, and after a while He was heard to sternly ordering him to publicly recognize his mistake and retract his words at once! "Go down and tell the people: I was like Saul. Now I am Paul, for I see."* Though reluctantly, Mr. MacNutt went down the stairs to the large assembly of believers and, "his back shrunken...", barely audible, went through his retraction. During this time... "the Master leaned over the stair rail, His head thrown far back, His eyes closed, in anguished prayer. This is like Christ in Gethsemane," Juliet thought.

When Howard MacNutt went up toward His room, 'Abdu'l-Bahá ran forward to meet him. "Our Lord was all in white that night

75

*J. P. Morgan Library, Madison Avenue and 36th Street: The main entrance used by 'Abdul'l-Bahá on November 18th, 1912.*

76

and as He ran arms wide open He looked like a great flying bird. He unfolded Howard in a close embrace welcomed with ecstasy this broken man who, though bewildered, had obeyed Him." The Master then called Mr. Kinney and others to His room and asked them to embrace Howard MacNutt, and from now on to work together teaching the Cause in perfect love and unity in the City of the Covenant.

"Obedience," the Master once said, "Obedience, is the rod by which I measure the love of the friends." The following night, someone gloated over Mr. MacNutt's chastisement. The Master sighed: "I immersed Mr. MacNutt in the fountain of Job last night."**

*    Reference to Biblical Saul of Tarsus who became Jesus' Apostle Paul after his vision on the Road to Damascus.
**   J. Thompson's Diary, pp. 369-72. Howard MacNutt's love and gratitude for the Master never failed after his ordeal. He went on as a dedicated teacher of his beloved Faith, until his and Mrs. Mary MacNutt's untimely death in a car accident.

*In the Guest Book of the J. P. Morgan Library: A prayer written by 'Abdul'l-Bahá for Mr. Morgan who died March 31, 1913. Translated by Dr. Fareed ("Farid" in American Bahá'í literature.)*

# THE DAY OF THE COVENANT

On November 20, 'Abdu'l-Bahá made a last visit to the home of Juliet and Mrs. Thompson. After resting in one of Juliet's room, He visited every room of the house and said: "This house is blessed." These words echoed in the heart of Juliet and her mother forever...

By spending Saturday, November 23, in Montclair, New Jersey, the Master missed the booking deadline for the S.S. Mauretania, to the delight of the friends. In the evening, the Day of the Covenant was celebrated with a great banquet at the Great Northern Hotel. The banquet room was magnificent; more than 300 Bahá'ís attended, some coming from the regions of Washington, Philadelphia and Boston. A few dignitaries such as Mr. Topakyan, were also invited. Before the food was served, 'Abdu'l-Bahá went among the guests, anointing everyone with attar of rose, a Persian custom to honor guests. The Master gave a short talk.

As the Great Northern Hotel manager had stubbornly and vehemently refused to allow black guests at the banquet, the friends organized a great interracial feast at the home of the Kinneys the following day. Many of the white ladies rose to serve the meal. The Master was very pleased and said: "Today you have shown the Commandments of the Blessed Beauty in your actions and have acted according to the teaching of the Supreme Pen." [40]

On November 25, 'Abdu'l-Bahá was the honored guest at the annual luncheon of the Club Minerva at the Waldorf Astoria hotel. Mrs. Mary MacNutt was the President of this renowned women's club. The Master spoke on the virtues and rights of women. He next visited the home of Mrs. Asa Cochran, where He gave a talk on the abolition of prejudices and on acquiring perfection through spiritual power.

Later, Juliet was at 'Abdu'l-Bahá's home waiting for the Master with Dr. Percy Grant, who had come for his farewell visit. The Master was happy to see Dr. Grant and apologized for keeping him waiting. He said, "I was captured by 300 women this afternoon. Is it not a dreadful thing?" They met in private in the Master's room. Dr. Farid, who was the interpreter, later told Juliet that Dr.Grant had expressed great concern for the safety of 'Abdu'l-Bahá who was going to a war area (Turkey and the Balkans) and had offered his services to help Him in any way he could, asking to be kept informed of His well-being.[41]

'Abdu'l-Bahá was born on May 23rd, 1844, on the same night the Báb, Forerunner of Bahá'u'lláh, revealed His Mission. In the early days of the Faith in Akka, the Master told the Persian friends, that this day was not to be celebrated as His birthday. It was the Day of the Declaration of the Báb, exclusively associated with Him. But, as the friends begged for a day to be celebrated as His, He gave them November 26th, to be observed as the day of the appointment of the Centre of the Covenant. It was known as the great Festival, because 'Abdu'l-Bahá was the Greatest Branch. In the West, it became known as the Day of the Covenant.*

In this context, the scene witnessed by Juliet on this November 26, 1912, in New York, takes a special significance.

On this Day of the Covenant, Juliet went to the home of Mr. and Mrs. Kinney to meet with 'Abdu'l-Bahá. He was on the upper floor with the Persian friends, Mr. Montford Mill, Carrie Kinney and others. Dr. Bagdadi and Dr. Farid were working on the official translation of The Tablet of The Branch under the stern supervision of 'Abdu'l-Bahá. The translation was submitted sentence by sentence to the Master until He was satisfied with the rendering. "I shall never forget... His sternness, His terrific majesty as he directed that translation." Throughout the proceedings, Juliet was overwhelmed and reacted with uncontrollable crying, comforted by Mahmud and Valíyu'lláh Khán, who understood her feelings.[42]

Future generations of Bahá'ís can only be grateful for Juliet Thompson's great love for 'Abdu'l-Bahá, and her sincerity, that He had praised. In her emotional testimony, we can see, unfolding within three days, the historical purpose of the Mystery of God in the City of the Covenant: June 19; November 18 and 26-events which can be remembered as the divine triptych which firmly established the continuity of the Faith of Bahá'u'lláh. **

*    From H.M. Balyuzi "'Abdu'l-Bahá," p.523.
**   During a 1980 pilgrimage in Haifa, this writer asked Hand of the Cause Mr. Furutan, if he knew the purpose of 'Abdu'l-Bahá in the City of the Covenant. Mr. Furutan explained that the Master had planned to build up the unity of the Bahá'ís in New York City to counter the destructive activities of the Covenant-breakers in Chicago. Mr. Furutan asserted: "Yes, and He stopped the Chicago Covenant-breakers from New York toward the end of His sojourn!" Also, at the Bahá'í International Archives, inquiry was made about the status of Juliet Thompson's diary. The friends were shown a package wrapped in brown paper and string with Shoghi Effendi's hand writing: "Diary of Juliet Thompson to be published in due time." And we were told "Shoghi Effendi loved it!"

*The House of Mrs. Asa Cochran visited by 'Abdul'l-Bahá on November 25th, 1912, is now a Fraternity House for Columbia University students. When Michel Samuel asked for permission to take this photograph, the students inquired about its purpose. Informed on 'Abdul'l-Bahá's visit and on the principles of the Faith, astonished, the students said that their Fraternity was for "Unity of People and of Culture", and they requested to be part of the photograph in homage to 'Abdul'l-Bahá and the lady who lived there.*

# FAREWELL!

During the last few days, the house of 'Abdu'l-Bahá was crowded with eager friends. The Master told them: "I always derive pleasure from our meetings. I shall always remember these days." The friends came to look at His face, "to turn to the Dawning Place of the Divine Covenant... He was imparting joy to the sad, hope to the hopeless and a flame to the dormant while He guided strugglers to the right path." At another time, the Master said, "... the purpose of the Holy Manifestations of God was not to found religions and churches, but to educate souls who will become teachers of mankind... The people of Bahá must endeavor day and night to enforce this divine purpose."

On that Thanksgiving Day, November 28, the Master expressed love for Americans and hope in their destiny to evolve toward spirituality with the same energy now directed toward material achievements.

Mr. and Mrs. Marshall Emery had invited 'Abdu'l-Bahá to move to their home for the last few days, but most of the large meetings were held at the Kinneys' until the end. Some of the friends wanted to offer money to the Master and gifts of jewelry for His relatives. He asked them to give everything to the poor. As the friends insisted, He said that He accepted their gifts, but they should sell them for His sake and give the proceeds to the fund for the construction of the House of Worship in Wilmette.

Speaking of impending international war, 'Abdu'l-Bahá expressed the wish that America would lead the world to peace and world unity. "In the religion of Bahá'u'lláh this question of peace is a positive command and a religious obligation... It is a positive divine command and is, thus, certain to come to pass."

At the home of Mr. and Mrs. Kinney on December 2, 'Abdu'l-Bahá announced His departure. "These are the days of my farewell

*Waldorf Astoria Hotel, Park Avenue, where 'Abdul'l-Bahá addressed Mrs. MacNutt's Club Minerva, on November 25th, 1912.*

to you, for I am sailing on the 5th of the month. Wherever I went in this country I returned always to New York City." The Master gave a beautiful exhortation ending with these words: "Be illumined, be spiritual, be divine, be glorious, be quickened of God, be a Bahá'í." [43]

This was not yet the end. In spite of all the final preparations, 'Abdu'l-Bahá continued to have meetings at the Kinneys', mostly with Bahá'ís. However, ministers and rabbis still sought to reach Him for guidance until the last day. His final public appearance was made the evening before His departure, at the Theosophical Society, where He delivered an address on the eternity of creation, the evolution of the spirit, and the power of the Manifestation of God.

Juliet had asked 'Abdu'l-Bahá for permission to stay "in some corner of His home" the entire day of December 4. She was allowed to do so although He was seeing many others. After everyone had left, the Master told Juliet that the proceeds of the sale of the photographs of His portrait that she had planned to send to the Temple fund were for her to keep. He was aware of Mrs. Thompson's and Juliet's dire financial situation since the death of her father. The portrait had been exhibited at the Church of the Ascension for several weeks, and now 'Abdu'l-Bahá was taking it with Him.*

On Thursday, December 5th, Juliet had gone early in the morning to the Emery's (last home of 'Abdu'l-Bahá in New York). She was trying to fill her memory with the Master's every move and expressions. The Master took her hand telling her, "Remember, I am with you always. Bahá'u'lláh will be with you always." He had expressed often these thoughts to the friends.

Juliet and some of the friends drove to the pier with the Master and followed Him up to His cabin on the S.S. Celtic. Then they all went to the large first class lounge, packed with Bahá'ís from various parts of the country. Walking back and forth, a familiar action when speaking to the friends, 'Abdu'l-Bahá gave them His last exhortation in the City of the Covenant, while all the friends were weeping quietly.

He reminded the friends that they were standing for the unity of all nations and for world peace while a war raged in the Balkans.

Then He said, "As to you, your efforts must be lofty. Exert yourselves with heart and soul that perchance through your efforts the light of Universal Peace may shine and this darkness of estrangement and enmity may be dispelled from amongst men.

"You have no excuse to bring before God if you fail to live according to His command, for you are informed of that which constitutes the good pleasure of God... It is my hope that you may become successful in this high calling, so that like brilliant lamps you may cast light upon the world of humanity and quicken and stir the body of existence like unto a spirit of life.

"This is eternal glory. This is everlasting felicity. This is immortal life. This is heavenly attainment. This is being created in God's image and likeness. And unto this I call you, praying God to strengthen and bless you." [44]

The passengers and officers of the Celtic were astonished at the scene: "Their surprise was beyond expression," noted Mahmud. "The Master was seated in a corner of the lounge, while the believers flocked around Him for the last minutes left." Juliet lamented, "... It was death to leave that ship. I stood on the pier with May Maxwell, tears blurred my sight. Through them, I could see the Master in the midst of the group of Persians waving a patient hand to us. It waved and waved, that beautiful hand, till the Figure was lost to sight."

From the ship, Mahmud could see the friends on the pier, "... the steamer moved out to sea, but as far as the eyes could see the multitude of the friends surged like a mighty host... The Beloved spoke about the power of the Greatest Name. 'Behold!' He said, 'By the power of the Cause of God a new spirit has been breathed into the hearts which has produced a change in the souls. Continuously the assistance of the Beauty of Abhá reached us and invariably the lights of victory shone from the Supreme Horizon. We received the confirmations of the Kingdom of God and the assistance of the Invisible Sovereignty of the Beauty of Abhá which He promised clearly in the verse:

'We see you from the horizon of Abhá and with the hosts of the Supreme Concourse and the armies of the Angels of Nearness We assist those who rise to help the Cause.'" [45]

---

\*    The original portrait has been lost. Only a few of the 1912 photographs are kept in private and Bahá'í archives. The illustration in this book is from one of these 1912 prints, from the estate of Mrs. Asa Cochran, courtesy of the Hopson-Samuel family

*Mr. and Mrs. Marshall Emery's house, last home of 'Abdu'l-Bahá in December, 1912. The Kinney family and other wealthy New York City Bahá'ís lost their fortune during the Depression. Their townhouses were sold and demolished and replaced by apartment buildings.*

# IN CONCLUSION

We may take the time to reflect on the extraordinary events that took place in this country in 1912 as they were part of a greater pattern.

In God Passes By, Shoghi Effendi, after relating the trials and sufferings of 'Abdu'l-Bahá and the recovery of His freedom, wrote: "So momentous a change in the fortune of the Faith was the signal for such an outburst of activity on His part as to dumbfound His followers in East and West with admiration and wonder, and exercise an imperishable influence on the course of its future history. He Who, in His own words, had entered prison as a youth and left it as an old man, Who never in His life had faced a public audience, had attended no school, had never moved in Western circles and was unfamiliar with Western customs and language, had arisen not only to proclaim from pulpit and platform in some of the chief capitals of Europe and in the leading cities of the North American continent, the distinctive verities enshrined in His Father's Faith, but to demonstrate as well the divine origin of the Prophets gone before Him and to disclose the nature of the tie binding them to that Faith."[46]

In this country, followed by throngs of Bahá'ís and anonymous people alike, and trailed by groups of astonished journalists and writers, 'Abdu'l-Bahá spoke to the lowliest of society and to the loftiest socialites, to leaders of thought and representatives of governments. He addressed large audiences, praising Christ in synagogues, bringing Mohammad's teachings to Christian churches and the unity of religion and science to universities, further proclaiming the Revelation of Bahá'u'lláh and His Mission of Peace to a world at the brink of world war. The Master nurtured the friends, one soul at a time, captivating new believers, confirming wavering ones, and made proud standard- bearers of the humblest, uniting all in the embracing shelter of His Divine Love.

Finally, The Mystery of God, 'Abdu'l-Bahá, unveiling the Spiritual Power of His Station as Center of the Covenant of Bahá'u'lláh, endowed New York with the imperishable title of "City of the Covenant."

The City of the Covenant
1987/1998

# THE SECOND BAHÁ'Í WORLD CONGRESS
## 23-26 November 1992

The 1992 World Congress was called by the Universal House of Justice to "celebrate the centenary of the inauguration of the Covenant of Bahá'u'lláh, and to proclaim its aims and unifying power." The World Congress was part of the Holy Year commemorating the centennial of the Ascension of Bahá'u'lláh and the site of the Congress was New York City, The City of the Covenant, as designated by 'Abdu'l-Bahá. The event lasted four days ending on the Day of the Covenant.

United States President George Bush sent his greetings from the White House and the Honorable Mario M. Cuomo, Governor of the State of New York, sent an official statement of welcome.

The Congress was officially opened by the Honorable David N. Dinkins, the (first black) Mayor of the City of New York, reading a Proclamation welcoming the international community of Bahá'ís, acknowledging the principles of the Faith, and evoking the Person of 'Abdu'l-Bahá who "visited New York City in 1912, calling it 'The City of the Covenant.'"

In response, Mayor Dinkins was presented with a framed reproduction of 'Abdu'l-Bahá's Prayer for the City of New York:

Bless Thou, O King of Kings, the City of New York! Cause the friends there to be kind to one another. Purify their souls and make their hearts to be free and detached. Illumine the world of their consciousness. Exhilarate their spirits and bestow celestial power and confirmation upon them. Establish there a heavenly realm, so that the City of Bahá may prosper and New York be favored with blessings from the Abhá Kingdom, that this region may become like the all-highest Paradise, may develop into a vineyard of God and be transformed into a heavenly orchard and a spiritual rose garden.

'Abdu'l Bahá

The Congress, beautifully organized, and incredibly awe-inspiring, was unforgettable for the nearly 30,000 Bahá'ís who participated, mostly from the Hemisphere and from around the world, many wearing their traditional dress.

Among the events attended, friends involved with the production of this book, were particularly moved by the " 'Abdu'l-Bahá's Mission to America" theme pavilion. The visitors were greeted by a life-size portrait of the Master reproducing the 1912 photograph opening this book. Spread out over five imposing rooms, large cut out dioramas of 1912 New York and panels of various enlarged photographs brought to life the Bahá'í scenes evoked in these pages. The visit concluded in a quiet room with the recording of 'Abdu'l-Bahá's voice.

'Abdu'l-Bahá's 1912 film was also part of the program.

# TABLETS AND LETTERS

## THE TABLET OF THE BRANCH

*On June 19, 1912, after the Proclamation of His Station, 'Abdu'l-Bahá asked one of His translators to read this Tablet of Bahá'u'lláh, referring to 'Abdu'l-Bahá as His successor, as confirmation of His Proclamation.*

*This Tablet's official translation into English was written under the Master's stern direction on the Day of the Covenant, November 26, and published in New York City on December 2, 1912 - three days before 'Abdu'l-Bahá's departure and distributed to the Bahá'í World Community.*

This has been revealed in Adrianople for Mirza Ali Riza in order that he may be nourished by the Favors of God.

He is Eternal in His Abhá Horizon!

Verily the Cause of God hath come upon the Clouds of Utterances and the polytheists are in this day in great torment. Verily the hosts of revelation have descended with banners of inspiration from the Heaven of the Tablet in the name of God, the Powerful, the Mighty. At this time the monotheists all rejoice in the victory of God and His dominion and the deniers will then be in manifest perplexity.

0 ye people! Do ye flee from the mercy of God after it has encompassed the existent things created between the heavens and earth? Beware lest ye prefer your own selves before the mercy of God, and deprive not yourselves thereof. Verily whosoever turneth away therefrom will be in great loss. Verily mercy is like unto verses which have descended from the one heaven and from them the monotheists drink the choice wine of Life, whilst the polytheists drink the fiery water (Hameen); and when the verses of God are read unto them, the fire of hatred is enkindled within their breasts. Thus

have they preferred their own selves before the mercy of God, and are of those who are heedless.

Enter, O people, beneath the shelter of the Word, then drink therefrom the choice wine of Inner Significances and Utterances; for therein is hidden the Kawther of the Glorious One-and it hath appeared from the horizon of the will of your Lord, the merciful, with wonderful lights.

Say: Verily the ocean of pre-existence hath branched forth from this most great ocean. Blessed therefore is he who abides upon its shores, and is of those who are established thereon. Verily this most sacred temple of Abhá-the Branch of Holiness-hath branched forth from the Sadratu'l-Muntaha. Blessed is whosoever hath sought shelter beneath it and is of those who rest therein.

Say: Verily the Branch of Command hath sprung forth from this root which God hath firmly planted in the ground of the will, the limb of which has been elevated to a station which encompasses all existence. Therefore exalted be he for this Creation, the Lofty, the Blessed, the Inaccessible, the Mighty!

O ye, people! draw nigh unto it (the Branch is referred to in this Tablet both as "It" and "His") and taste the fruits of its knowledge and wisdom on the part of the Mighty, the Knowing One. Whosoever will not taste thereof shall be deprived of the bounty, even though he has partaken of all that is in the earth - were ye of those who know.

Say: Verily a word hath gone forth from the Most Great Tablet and God hath adorned it with the mantle of Himself and made it sovereign over all on the earth and a sign of His grandeur and omnipotence among the creatures; in order that, through it, the people shall praise their Lord the mighty, the powerful, the wise; and that, through it, they shall glorify their Creator and sanctify the self of God which standeth within all things. Verily this is naught but a revelation upon the part of the Wise, the Ancient One! Say: O people, praise ye God for its manifestation (the Branch), for verily it (the Branch) is the most great favor upon you and the most perfect blessing upon you; and through Him every mouldering bone is quickened. Whosoever turns to Him hath surely turned unto God and whosoever turneth away from Him hath turned away from my beauty, denied my proof, and is of those who transgress. Verily, He is the remembrance of God amongst you and His trust within you and His manifestation unto you and His appearance among the servants who are nigh. Thus have I been commanded to convey to you the message of God, your Creator; and I have delivered to you that of which I was commanded. Whereupon, thereunto testifieth God, then His angels, then His messengers, and then His holy servants.

Inhale the fragrances of the Ridván from His roses and be not of those who are deprived. Appreciate the bounty of God upon you and be not veiled therefrom - and verily we have sent Him forth in the temple of man. Thus praise ye the Lord, the Originator of whatsoever He willeth through His wise and inviolable command!

Verily, those who withhold themselves from the Shelter of the Branch are indeed lost in the wilderness of perplexity - and are consumed by the heat of self-desire - and are of those who perish.

Hasten, O people, unto the Shelter of God, in order that He may protect you from the heat of the day whereon none shall find for himself any refuge or shelter except beneath the shelter of His Name, the clement, the forgiving. Clothe yourselves, O people, with the garment of assurance, in order that He may protect you from the darts of doubts and superstitions, and that ye may be of those who are assured in those days wherein none shall ever be assured and none shall be firmly established in the Cause except by severing himself from all that is possessed by the people and turning unto the holy and radiant outlook.

O ye people! Do ye take unto yourselves the Jebt (an idol) as a helper other than God, and do ye seek the Taghoot (an idol) as a Lord besides your Lord the Almighty, the Omnipotent? Forsake, O people, their mention, then hold the Chalice of Life in the name of your Lord the Merciful. Verily by God, the existent world is quickened through a drop thereof, were ye of those who know.

Say: In that day there is no refuge for any one save the command of God, and no salvation for any soul but God. Verily this is the truth and there is naught after truth but manifest error.

Verily God hath made it incumbent upon every soul to deliver His Cause (the Message) according to his ability. Thus hath the command been recorded by the finger of might and power upon the Tablet of majesty and greatness.

Whosoever quickens one soul in this Cause is like unto one quickening all the servants and the Lord shall bring him forth in the Day of Resurrection into the Ridván of Oneness, adorned with the mantle of Himself, the Protector, the Mighty, the Generous. Thus will ye assist your Lord, and naught else save this shall ever be mentioned in this day before God your Lord and the Lord of your forefathers.

As to thee, 0 servant: hearken unto the admonition given unto thee in the Tablet; then seek the grace of thy Lord at all times. Then spread the Tablet among those who believe in God and in His verses; so that they may follow that which is contained therein, and be of those who are praiseworthy.

Say: 0 people, cause no corruption in the earth and dispute not with men; for verily this is not worthy of those who have chosen in the shelter of their Lord a station which shall indeed remain secure.

If ye find one athirst, give him to drink from the Chalice of Kawtha and Tasneen; and if ye find one endowed with an attentive ear, read unto him the verses of God, the Mighty, the Merciful, the Compassionate! Unloose the tongue with excellent utterance, then admonish the people if ye find them advancing unto the sanctuary of God, otherwise abandon them unto themselves and forsake them in the abyss of hell. Beware lest ye scatter the pearls of Inner Significance before every barren, dumb one. Verily the blind are deprived of witnessing the Lights and are unable to distinguish between the stone and the holy, precious pearl.

Verily, wert thou to read the most mighty, wonderful verses to the stone for a thousand years, will it understand, or will they take any effect therein? No! by thy Lord the Merciful, the Clement! If thou readest all the verses of God unto the deaf, will he hear a single letter? No! Verily by the Beauty, the Mighty, the Ancient!

Thus have we delivered unto thee some of the jewels of Wisdom and Utterance, in order that thou mayest gaze unto the direction of thy Lord and be served from all the creatures. May the Spirit and Glory rest upon thee, and upon those who dwell upon the plain of holiness and who remain in the cause of their Lord in manifest steadfastness!

# TABLETS FROM 'ABDU'L-BAHA

Tablets and letters from 'Abdu'l-Bahá addressed to the New York City Community compiled from " 'Abdu'l-Bahá in New York" a 1932 book now out of print.

Thou Compassionate Lord: This Assembly has been organized for the exaltation of God-the Holy Spirit. Assist, confirm it and reinforce it by Thy heavenly power so that it may blaze like unto a brilliant flame and may diffuse merciful light, that it may illumine the surrounding regions, may promulgate heavenly teachings and serve the oneness of the world of mankind, that it may free the souls from the darkness of the world of nature, may illumine them by the divine light, may baptize them with spirit and may bestow light and eternal life.

\* \* \* \* \*

Deliver my greeting and praise and my abundant longings to my beloved ones in that city (New York) which hath become the City of the Covenant, and the town of the love of God. The signs thereof will surely appear as the sun at midday. Truly I say unto thee, I love the beloved ones in that city with all my heart and soul, for as much as they love union, harmony and accord and are firm in resisting the people of discord and hypocrisy. Verily this is one of the greatest favors on the part of God and one of the mightiest bounties from the presence of God.

The good news of the unity and concord of the friends in New York proved a great source of joy. The original intention and the divine foundation is the unification of the world of humanity.

Therefore, this merciful reality must first find realization among the friends so that it may affect other souls.

* * * * *

Today the world and the people are under the shadow of Divine Providence: the light of the Sun of Reality has been shed upon the world of minds and thoughts: hence, light is seen everywhere.

O ye who are sincere! O ye who are firm! O ye who have risen to the service of the Cause of God and to the exaltation of His Word among mankind!

Happy are ye, for you have established a spiritual assembly under the shadow of your Lord's protection, who is the most compassionate and merciful, and have sought to diffuse the fragrances of God in those regions. In doing this, you have no other motive than to draw near unto God and secure a place in His magnificent Kingdom, till you receive more and more confirmation by the breath of the Holy Spirit in this glorious age.

And I tell you the truth, that if you remain firm in this path and if this luminous assembly continues to exist soon shall it possess transcendent signs, radiant rays of light and sweet fragrances, which will fill all sides of that exalted country with refreshing perfumes. And verily God will assist you with a power which will bewilder the wise, but which will dilate your breasts with joy at every moment. Before long shall you see that that assembly shall surpass high assemblies of former dispensations. So be ye firm and steadfast and manfully face all intensely trying ordeals. Strive not to indulge in scandalous gossip, even though it assumes a different form, for it shall vanish while your service to the Cause of God shall remain, just as shall remain your mention in the Tablets of the exalted Kingdom.

* * * * *

O ye who are turned toward the Kingdom and drawn unto the Holy Fragrances diffused from the Garden of El-Abhá.

Arise with every power to assist the Covenant of God and serve in His vineyard. Be confident that a confirmation will be granted unto you and a success on His part given unto you. Verily He shall support you by the angels of His Holiness and reinforce with the breaths of the Spirit that ye may mount the Ark of Safety, set forth the evident signs, impart the spirit of life, declare the essence of His commands and precepts, guide the sheep who are straying from the fold in all directions, use every effort in your power to give the blessings ye have and strive earnestly and wisely in this new century. By God, verily the Lord of Hosts is your support, the angels of heaven your assistance, the Holy Spirit your companion and the Center of the Covenant your helper! Be not idle, but active and fear not. Look unto those who have lived in the former ages how they have resisted all nations and suffered persecutions and afflictions, and how their stars shone and their attacks proved successful, their teachings established, their regions expanded, their hearts gladdened, their ideas cleared and their motives effective. Ye are now in a great station and noble rank and ye shall find yourselves in evident success and prosperity, the like of which the eye of existence hath never seen in former ages.

El-Abhá and salutations be upon everyone who is firm in the Covenant, free from dissension, sanctified from deceits and steadfast in the path!

\* \* \* \* \*

I am greatly pleased with the city of New York. The harbor entrance, its piers, buildings and broad avenues are magnificent and beautiful. Truly it is a wonderful city. As New York has made such progress in material civilization, I hope that it may also advance spiritually in the Kingdom and Covenant of God, so that the friends here may become the cause of the illumination of America: that this city may become the city of love and that the fragrances of God may be spread from this place to all parts of the world. I have come for this.

* * * * *

**Prayer revealed for the New York Bahá'í Community**

O my God! O my God! Verily Thou seest those who are present here turning to Thee, supplicating Thee, relying upon Thee.

O my Lord! O my Lord! Illumine their eyes by the light of guidance, and brighten their hearts with the rays shining from the Supreme Concourse. Suffer them to become the signs of Thy bestowal amongst the people, the standards of Thy power within mankind. O Lord, make those who are here the hosts of heaven and subdue through their means the hearts of mankind. Cause Thy great mercy to descend upon them, and render all Thy friends victorious through Thy love. Continually may they turn to the kingdom of Thy Names, and proclaim Thy Name amongst the people. May they attract all to the Pathway of Thy most great guidance.

O Lord! O Lord! Ordain for them honor in Thy kingdom of eternity.

O Lord! O Lord! Protect them from every test and make their feet firm in Thy love. Suffer them to be as strong, mighty mountains in Thy Cause, so that their steps shall not waver and their sight shall not be clouded and hindered from witnessing the lights emanating from Thy Supreme kingdom.

Verily Thou art the generous; verily, Thou art the almighty, verily, Thou art the clement, the merciful!

* * * * *

Strive you day and night that you may establish the power of the Covenant. Today the power that is able to quicken the heart of the world is the power of the Covenant. As the believers of God in New York, praise be to God, have found a new power in the Covenant and Testament, therefore they have gained happiness, attraction and motion.

The more the Covenant is established, the more the power of the Holy Spirit will become manifest.

Truly, I say, if the believers of God become united with heart and soul, in a short time they will shine forth like unto the sun. They will obtain joy and happiness-the splendor of which will be cast upon all the regions of America.

New York is the candle of America, but on account of discord and differences of opinion, it had become extinguished. Now, praise be to God, it is illumined again. My hope is such that New York may become so luminous that it may illumine all the American continent. Now that unity is established, undoubtedly the confirmations of God and infinite assistance will be obtained.

Every one of the friends who travels to America reaches New York first, and hastens to the assembly of the friends.

Should he become intoxicated from the chalice of unity, he would travel in that country as if he were dancing with joy. But otherwise, unquestionable, he would become depressed and dispirited. In short, for the friends in New York, I beseech heavenly bounty and spiritual confirmations.

\* \* \* \* \*

I have stayed in New York a long time. Although at times I went away, I have always returned to New York, because I wished New York to advance greatly. In former times New York was the Bahá'í center. It had precedent over other cities from every standpoint, even in point of numbers. I would like to see New York now as it was formerly, that is, with many friends. I would like to see this assembly increase day by day, and this is contingent upon one thing, that is, you must set aside all differences and become one in thought. This is the call of the Kingdom of Abhá. When water is distributed through various channels or founts, none of the fountains shall have sufficient strength and power, all of them will be meager. But when you shut off the sources and force the water in one direction, you will see a tremendous outflow. Even so it is with the thought of mankind. When human thought is not centered, it is working here and elsewhere; no thought force will be strong, but if you shut off all other forces and make all as one thought, there will be a tremendous power in that one direction. Therefore, you must forsake all thoughts, be united, set aside all intentions and hold only to one intention. This is the summons to the Kingdom of Abhá. This is the invitation to the Great Kingdom of the Lord. If this is accomplished, New York in the course of a year, will become bright; it will become fragrant; it will become a rose-garden; it will be delightful. The rays of the Sun of Light will shine. The faces will be most happy. Human realities will develop, that station of revelation and discovery will be attained, and the Stars of God will become resplendent.

Consider how all the people are asleep and ye are awake. They are dead and ye are alive through the breaths of the Holy Spirit. They are blind while ye are endowed with perceptive sight. They are deprived of the love of God but in your hearts it exists and is glowing. Consider these bestowals and favors.

Therefore in thanksgiving for them, ye must act in accordance with the teachings of Bahá'u'lláh. Ye must read the Tablets, Hidden Words, Ishrakhat, Glad Tidings -all the Holy Utterances, and act according to them. This is real thanksgiving, to live in accord with these utterances. This is true thankfulness and the divine bestowal. This is thanksgiving and glorification of God.

I hope you all may attain thereto, be mindful of these favors of God and be attentive. It is my hope that I may go away from New York with a happy heart, and my heart is happy when the friends of God love each other; when they manifest the mercy of God to all people.

\* \* \* \* \*

Souls from the East and the West have been brought together here through the power of the Holy Spirit. Such a gathering as this would be impossible through material means. A meeting of this kind has now been established in New York, for here tonight we find people from remote regions of the earth, associated with the people of America in the utmost love and spiritual unity. This is only possible through the power of God.

* * * * *

## Meeting of the Board of Council:

It is my hope that the meetings of the Bahá'í Assembly in New York shall become like meetings of the Supreme Concourse. When you assemble you must reflect the lights of the heavenly kingdom. Let your hearts be as mirrors in which the radiance of the Sun of Reality is visible. Each bosom must be a telegraph station; one terminus of the wire attached to the soul, the other fixed in the Supreme Concourse, so that inspiration may descend from the Kingdom of Abhá and questions of reality be discussed. Then opinion will coincide with truth; day by day there will be progression and the meetings become more radiant and spiritual. This attainment is conditioned upon unity and agreement. The more perfect the love and agreement, the more the divine confirmations and assistance of the Blessed Perfection will descend. May this prove to be a divine meeting and may boundless bestowals come down upon you. Strive with all your hearts and with the very power of life that unity and love may continually increase. In discussions look toward the reality without being self opinionated. Let no one assert and insist upon his own mere opinion; nay rather, let each investigate the reality with the greatest love and fellowship. Consult upon every matter and when one presents the point of view of the reality itself, that shall be acceptable to all. Then will spiritual unity increase among you, individual illumination will be greater, happiness more abundant and you will draw nearer and nearer to the kingdom of God.

* * * * *

I desire distinction for you. The Bahá'ís must be distinguished from others of humanity. But this distinction must not depend upon wealth - that they should become more affluent than other people. I do not desire for you financial distinction. It is not an ordinary distinction I desire; not scientific, commercial, industrial distinction. For you I desire spiritual distinction; that is, you must become eminent and distinguished in morals. In the love of God you must become distinguished from all else. You must become distinguished for loving humanity; for unity and accord; for love and justice. In brief, you must become distinguished in all the virtues of the human world; for faithfulness and sincerity; for justice and fidelity; for firmness and steadfastness; for philanthropic deeds and service to the human world; for love toward every human being; for unity and accord with all people; for removing prejudices and promoting international peace. Finally, you must become distinguished for heavenly illumination and acquiring the bestowals of God. I desire this distinction for you. This must be the point of distinction among you.

\* \* \* \* \*

O ye elect and chosen ones of the Kingdom!

Thank God that the Greatest Name selected and elected that gathering, ushered it into the Kingdom of Eternal Glory, honoured and crowned it amid the Supreme Concourse.

He placed upon each head a glorious diadem of guidance and established each one upon the throne of eternal reign. This is not known now but shall become evident and clear hereafter.

The seed when growing, at first doth not attract attention, but later it becometh green and thriveth, adorning the rose-garden and the orchard. Now, likewise, this divine bounty is unknown, it is not yet revealed, but soon will its splendour illumine the horizons and brighten the East and the West.

\* \* \* \* \*

I have been in your gatherings many times. I have not attended one-tenth of the number of meetings in other cities which I have attended in this city, but with you I have been in meetings day times, during evenings, with you individually, with you collectively and I have told you the teachings and exhortations of His Holiness Bahá'u'lláh. I conveyed unto you the glad tidings of God, I explained unto you the wishes of the Blessed Perfection; that which is conducive to human progress have I explained to you, and that which leads to the most great humility. I have given you a thorough explanation of the teachings of Bahá'u'lláh.

\* \* \* \* \*

I hope that the Northeastern States, especially New York, may attain to the utmost state of perfection in the cause of God, and in the matter of teaching and the promotion of the Word of God, they may precede the friends of other parts. New York is the first and greatest city of the Western Hemisphere and the numberless passengers who come to America, come and pass through this city. Therefore, its important position is quite secure and must be taken into consideration. The friends of this city must be in the utmost love and amity, so that their unity may serve as an example to the other States.

\* \* \* \* \*

O ye beloved friends of 'Abdu'l-Bahá!

You have written that there is a difference among believers concerning the "Second Coming of Christ." Praise be to God! - time and again this question hath arisen and its answer hath emanated in a clear and irrefutable text from the pen of 'Abdu'l-Bahá that what is meant in the prophecies by the "Lord of Hosts," the "Promised Christ" is the Blessed Perfection (Bahá'u'lláh) and His Highness the Supreme (the Báb). The faith of everyone must revolve around this palpable and evident text.

107

My name is 'Abdu'l-Bahá, my identity is 'Abdu'l-Bahá, my qualification is 'Abdu'l-Bahá, my reality is 'Abdu'l-Bahá, my praise is 'Abdu'l-Bahá. Thralldom to the Blessed Perfection is my glorious and refulgent diadem; and servitude to all the human race is my perpetual religion. Through the bounty and favour of the Blessed Perfection, 'Abdu'l-Bahá is the ensign of the Most-Great-Peace, which is waving from the supreme apex; and through the gift of the Greatest Name he is the Lamp of Universal Salvation, which is shining with the light of the love of God. The Herald of the Kingdom is he, so that he may awaken the people of the East and of the West. The Voice of Friendship, Uprightness, Truth and Reconciliation is he, so as to cause acceleration throughout all regions. No name, no title, no mention, no commendation hath he nor will ever have except 'Abdu'l-Bahá. This is my longing. This is my supreme apex. This is my greatest yearning. This is my eternal life. This is my everlasting glory! Express ye the same thing which is issued from my pen. This is the duty of all. Consequently the friends of God must assist and help 'Abdu'l-Bahá in the adoration of the True One; in the servitude to the human race; in the well-being of the human world and in divine love and kindness.

O ye friends of God! Through the appearance of the Blessed Perfection the theories are abrogated and the facts are established. The time of superficiality is gone by and the cycle of reality hath appeared. One must become the incarnation of servitude, the personification of love, the embodiment of spirituality and the mirror of mercy.

The believers must become the cause of life; deliver the people from heedlessness, call the souls to the perfection of humanity, beckon nations to unity and agreement, destroy the foundation of foreignness, make everyone as friends and associates, treat the negligent souls as their own children and train and educate them with the utmost love -so that the ignorant become wise, the blind become endowed with sight, and the deaf be given hearing.

O ye friends of God, beware! Beware of differences! By differences the Temple of God is razed to its very foundation, and by the blowing of the winds of disagreement the Blessed Tree is prevented from bearing any fruit. By the intense cold of the diversity of opinions the rose-garden of unity is withered, and the fire of the love of God is extinguished!

O ye friends of God! 'Abdu'l-Bahá is the Manifestation of Thralldom and not "Christ." The servant of the human realm is he and not a "chief." Non-existent is he and not "Existent." Pure nothingness is he and not "Eternal."

There is no outcome or result to these discussions. We must put aside these disputes and controversies, nay rather must we consign them to utter oblivion and arise to do that which is indispensable and which is demanded of us in this day. Controversies are words and not significances, theories and not realities.

The quintessence of truth is this: We must all become united and harmonized in order to illumine this gloomy world, to abolish the foundations of hostility and animosity from among mankind, to perfume the inhabitants of the universe with the holy fragrances of the nature and disposition of the beauty of Abhá, to enlighten the people of the East and West with the light of guidance, to hoist the tenet of the love of God and suffer each and all to enter under its protection, to bestow comfort and tranquility on everyone under the shade of the Divine Tree, to astonish the enemy by the manifestation of the utmost love, to make the ravenous and blood-thirsty wolves to be gazelles of the meadow of the love of God; to administer the taste of non-resistance to the tyrant, to teach long-suffering and resignation of the martyrs to the murderer, to spread the traces of oneness, to chant the praises and glorification of the glorious Lord, to raise the voice of "Ya Bahá El-Abhá! " to the supreme apex and to reach the ears of the inhabitants of the Kingdom with the outcry. This is reality! This is guidance! This is service! This is the consummation of the perfection of the realm of humanity!

O ye believers of God! Each person must summon the people to the servitude of 'Abdu'l-Bahá and not the Christhood, and no soul must either publicly or privately utter one word against or in contradiction to the general teachings, and no one must believe that

'Abdu'l-Bahá is the "Second Coming of Christ," nay, rather he must believe that he is the manifestation of servitude, the mainspring of the unity of the human world, the herald of the True One with spiritual power throughout all regions, the commentator of the Book according to the divine text, and the ransom to each one of the believers of God in the transitory world.

Print ye this tablet and spread it throughout all countries.

\* \* \* \* \*

O, ye sons of the Kingdom!

Your letter was received and from the contents of the report the utmost of joy was obtained, for it indicated firmness and was a proof of your arising to serve.

When the intention is for God, ultimately the object is attained, unity and accord will appear.

I am hopeful that when I come to those regions and meet the friends perfect unity and accord will ensue.

Praise be to God in Paris and London there is not a trace of discord. They are in perfect accord and agreement; all are engaged in service. Day by day they are advancing spiritually, and are guiding new souls. The good leaves, the ladies who returned from Europe have certainly detailed the account.

The circle of friendship among the human race must be enlarged and (you) must associate and unite with the good souls who have no purpose save goodness and are striving for Universal Peace and desire the solidarity and the oneness of the human world. They must awaken them in regard to the Divine Kingdom, for their intentions are good but they do not know that the powers in the world are incapable of establishing the Universal Peace and promulgating the oneness of the world of man save through the power of the word of God and the breath of the Holy Spirit. This power alone can remove differences, warfare and strife from among (the people) inasmuch as the Congress of Universal Peace and the Unity of the Races are radiant but are like the candles; a limited circle only do they illuminate, but the whole world is now made radiant through the rise of the Sun of Truth and darkness is entirely dispelled. This matter must be known to those important souls in the Congress for International Peace.

Consider how many conferences for philanthropy were held in the olden times, people braving difficulties and the utmost ordeals but their benefits were limited, but the rise of the light of Truth and the morn of Guidance through the power of the Holy Spirit affords unlimited benefits. Therefore in good intentions you must seek help from the boundless Power.

* * * * *

My Lord the Helper of every assembly gathered for the exaltation of the Word of Thy Mercy and the Strengthener of every party that agreed to the service of the Threshold of Thy Oneness:

I ask Thee by Thy Beauty which is secreted in Thy Brilliant (Abhá) Unseen Worlds, that the Favor of the Eye of Thy Mercy may embrace them and strengthen them with most Mighty Power, and to gird up their loins by Thy Power which is victoriously successful in all things.

Verily, Thou art the hearer of prayer and verily, Thou art the powerful above all thing.

In this day, the gathering of a board for consultation is of great importance and a great necessity. For all, obedience to it is a necessity, especially because the members (of the Board) are the hand of the Cause.

So they (the members) must confer and consult in such a way that neither disagreement nor abhorrence may occur. When meeting for consultation, each must use perfect liberty in stating his views and unveiling the proof of his demonstration. If another contradicts him, he must not become excited because if there be no investigation or verifications of questions and matters, the agreeable view will not be discovered neither understood. The brilliant light which comes from the collision of thoughts is the "lightener" of facts.

If all views are in harmony at the end of a conference, it will be excellent; but if - God forbid! - disagreement occurs, then the decision must be according to the greater number in harmony. If, after reaching the result, one or the others of the members does not agree with it, neither of the other members nor any one must argue with or reproach him, but keep silence; then they will write to this Servant (the Master).

None (of the members of the board) must spread the matters or methods pertaining to the conference. At the opening of the conference they are to ask God for special assistance and help and for their Ruler and his assistants and for the Governors of the Country.

During the conference no hint must be entertained regarding political affairs. All conferences must be regarding the matters of benefit, both as a whole and individually, such as the guarding of all in all cases, their protection and preservation, the improvement of character, the training of children, etc.

If any person (soul) wishes to speak of government affairs, or to interfere with the order of Governors, the others must not combine with him (in such a matter) because the cause of God is withdrawn entirely from political affairs; the political realm pertains only to the Rulers of those matters; it has nothing to do with the souls who are exerting their utmost energy to harmonizing affairs, helping character and inciting (the people) to strive for perfections. Therefore no soul is allowed to interfere with (political) matters, but only in that which is commanded.

\* \* \* \* \*

O, ye chosen ones! O, ye heralds! O, ye advancing ones! O, ye deliverers of the Truth! Verily I stretch out the hands of supplication to God, that He may confirm you in serving the Word of God, in His Great Vineyard, so that ye may spread the Signs of God, explain His Proofs and arguments and demonstrate the Manifestation of His Kingdom among the Creatures.

Know ye! Verily your assembly is under the Protection of God and your persons are favored by the glances of the Eyes of Mercifulness. Make firm your feet, be steadfast in the Cause of God, trust in God and rely upon His confirmations under all circumstances.

Verily your Lord has chosen you from among the multitude and hath assisted you through His Angels, so that ye may arise with all your powers in diffusing the Fragrances of God, protecting the Word of God, guiding the souls, training the minds and establishing the Religion of God in those parts.

This is a Bounty which nothing equals, even the Kingdom of the whole earth. But at present it is concealed from eyes and its value is not known except to the people of discernment among the righteous; verily they see it great and glorious! Its greatness, exaltation and loftiness shall surely appear throughout all regions.

Reflect upon the Disciples of Christ in the early centuries. The people did not care for their Assemblage, the power of their hosts nor for the greatness of their station, nay they supposed them as the (ordinary) people. But before a long time had elapsed, their augmentation appeared, their signs were promulgated, their Fragrances were diffused, their lights shone forth throughout all parts.

As to you, O, ye chosen ones! Use all your endeavors concerning your spiritual meeting and be steadfast in the Divine Cause. If people despise you be not grieved, nay rather grow in firmness and steadfastness in this Cause; so that you may find the Angels of Heaven assisting you and the Holy Spirit strengthening you in every important and momentous matter.

Upon ye be greeting and praise!

\* \* \* \* \*

O ye beloved friends of 'Abdu'l-Bahá: The news of your spiritual assembly reached this Illumined Spot and the heart of this yearning One was rejoiced on account of your concord, unity and affinity. What wonderful meetings and brilliant gatherings were those - whose fame will become world-wide and whose melody will ere long reach to all the Kingdoms, that in the regions of America the believers are real companions and associates with each other and are as beloved friends among themselves, that they bring about gatherings of friendship, engage themselves in the praise and glorification of the Glorious Lord, deliver eloquent speeches, establish the proofs and arguments of the Manifestation of the Sun of Truth, spread the Divine Teachings and shed broadcast the musk-diffusing Fragrances of the Kingdom; - so that the nostrils become perfumed and the eyes become brightened.

O ye friends! O ye maid-servants of the Merciful!

Those assemblies are the emblems of the Supreme Concourse and the prototypes of the Congregations of the spirits in the Abhá Kingdom. Avail yourselves of the opportunities of this time, neither let the occasion slip by unheeded. The season of the soul-refreshing spring will not appear at all times, neither will the breezy dawn be at every moment. Now is the time of proclamation and the occasion of supplication and invocation toward the Kingdom of Abhá.

Therefore, sing ye with the sweet melody in the assemblages, entreat ye at the Threshold of the Kingdom of the Lord of Hosts and beg ye for Confirmation and assistance. The Guide of Providence will appear and the Beloved of Divine Gifts will unveil her luminous countenance.

Upon you be Bahá El-Abhá!

* * * * *

O ye who are persevering in the service of the Cause of God! O ye who are sincere in the religion of God! O ye who are mentioned in this merciful assembly through the Bounty of God!

Verily, by day and by night I mention you, and will not forget you in the mornings nor in the evenings.

I supplicate God to uphold you with a Divine Power, heavenly might, merciful confirmations, and everlasting success, that ye may become luminous lamps; spreading the lights of knowledge to the people of the contingent world, and proclaiming the Name of God, saying, "the doors of the Kingdom have been opened before the face of every man; the sea of favors has moved, casting the pearls of gifts on the sides of the hearts and spirits; and the Sun of the Most Great Gift has shone in these days, from which dazzling rays are abundantly sent to all regions."

O ye friends of the Merciful! be tranquil and have all confidence that the mercy of God shall surround you from all sides, and the Spiritual Breath shall quicken your spirits at every minute and time. Therefore, God be thanked for these heavenly gifts, these unseen favors, and these merciful abundances.

It is incumbent upon you not to be remiss in exalting the Word of God by day and by night. Be severed from the world and turn your faces to the Most Great Grace in the Kingdom of heaven, that the Mighty One may uphold you with the greatest gifts in this first growth.

Send monthly reports of the minutes of that Spiritual Assembly, that constant communications might continue between the Blessed Spot and that Spiritual Assembly.

May salutations and praise be upon you.

*****

O, ye faithful ones! O, ye chosen ones! O, ye attracted ones! 0, ye who have arisen to the service of the Cause of God, and the promulgation of His Word among the inhabitants of the world!

I supplicate to God that He will make your gathering-place a glorious Tabernacle, a holy Throne, and a center of the divine emotions; so that you may become luminous lamps, and that from your faces radiate the lights of guidance among mankind, that you may hear the Call of the Almighty from the Supreme Concourse, opening your mouths in the glorification of the Beauty of Abhá, spreading divine teachings in that vast country, and educating humanity with heavenly education which conduces to the quickening of the souls and spirits.

By the life of Truth, I say with you, verily the Hosts of the Supreme Concourse are ranked expecting the time that the glorious personages move forward in the Place of the love of God, and arise to help the Cause of God, in order that the Angels of Holiness confirm them with divine and unheard of power.

Hasten ye! Hasten ye! O, ye righteous ones! Hasten ye, Hasten ye, O, ye chosen ones! Hasten ye, Hasten ye, O, ye intelligent ones! Avail the opportunity! Do not expend one eye's wink uselessly in this heavenly Rose-Garden, until you behold that the Doors of the Bounty are opened before your faces, and the lamps of Guidance ignited in your hearts.

Verily your Lord is the Merciful, the Compassionate, the Bestower!

\* \* \* \* \*

In brief, whenever you witness in any soul the image and likeness of God, know ye of a certainty that he (or she) is a Bahá'í, that is, the signs of the effulgences of Bahá'u'lláh, are revealed in him; the sanctification and purity of Bahá'u'lláh, the virtues of Bahá'u'lláh, the perfections of Bahá'u'lláh, and the might and dominion of Bahá'u'lláh. Whenever you witness the rays of His bestowal in any soul, the image and likeness of Bahá'u'lláh reflected, know that he assuredly is a Bahá'í, that he is the servant of Bahá'u'lláh, that he is related to Bahá'u'lláh, he is the sign of Bahá'u'lláh. Otherwise he is not at all related to Bahá'u'lláh. Bahá'u'lláh is free from him; He has nothing to do with him.

Therefore, strive, have no rest day or night, until you attain to the characteristics of the angelic kingdom. May you become the signs of guidance. May you become the lamps of the Kingdom of God. May you become shining stars in the Kingdom of Everlasting Glory. May you illumine the world of humanity. May you become the very spirit of the world of humanity, so that the world may be likened unto a body and you the spirit animating that body. May you bestow life. May you illumine. May you enlighten. These are the characteristics of the people of Bahá. This is the behavior of the people of Bahá. These are the aims of the people of Bahá. It is my hope that all of you may become assisted and confirmed therein. Praise be to God, you are all under the shade of His protection!

Praise be to God, that you are surrounded with the glance of his mercifulness! Praise be to God, that you are related to Him! Praise be to God, that you are receiving lights from His Sun! Ere long you shall witness that the rays of the Sun of Bahá'u'lláh have illumined the Orient and the Occident.

\* \* \* \* \*

O ye faithful, O ye sincere!

Verily, in the midst of nights and with a heart overflowing with fervent supplications and earnest prayers, 'Abdu'l-Bahá beseeches his Lord to shower down upon you the divine gifts of the heavenly table, that ye may rejoice through His bounty, munificence and the abundance of His Lights and be illumined by the sun of His Reality, the dawn of which is dazzling upon the East and the West.

O beloved of God! Great, great is the matter! Illustrious, illustrious is the victory! Glorious, glorious is the Age! Steady, steady is the abundance, and the lights have encompassed all regions.

Arise with divine power, merciful intention, heavenly zeal, spiritual character, resolute aim, and rely upon God, the Peerless, endeavor in the service of the Cause of God, put every effort in the vineyard of God, utter the praise of God, spread the fragrances of God, characterize yourselves with the characteristics of God, clothe yourselves with the vestments of angels, and adorn yourselves with the excellences of merit which is the real ornament of man.

Be the guideposts of favor, the banners of perfection, the lighthouses of science and knowledge, the standards of unity and the signs of the gift of the glorious Lord. This is that whereby your faces would be illumined in the Supreme World and your breasts dilated with joy through the favors of the Lord of the Sublime Heaven.

O ye sons and daughters of the Kingdom!

Your letter of felicitation (November 26, 1913) was received. Its contents were the proof of your firmness, and evidence that you have turned your faces toward the Kingdom of Abhá, holding fast to the Covenant and that your hearts are attracted by the Orb of regions.

Today all the nations of the world are submerged in the darkness of ignorance and the superstitious religious, racial patriotic and political prejudices, but the lights of the oneness of the world of humanity are shining and irradiating from your faces, and the fire of the love of God is ignited and set aglow in your hearts.

Praise be to God that you have no other aim save the Unity of mankind, entertain no other hope except the guidance of all the people and harbor no other wish save the good pleasure of the Lord. I hope that you may become so illumined as to enlighten all the regions; each one of you may become a bright candle, the sign of the Love of God, the herald of the Kingdom of God, the means of communication between the hearts of all humanity and be confirmed for bringing about the confederation of all the religions; - so that this dark world may become luminous, the foundation of warfare and battle be utterly destroyed, the standard of Universal Peace be upraised in the center of the world and the Feast of Love be spread amongst the children of men.

With the utmost humility and meekness I supplicate and implore in your behalf toward the Kingdom of Abhá and beg confirmation for you - so that the City of New York may become the center of the Most Great Guidance and the lights may be scattered to all parts of the world from the hearts of the believers!

* * * * *

O ye sons of the Kingdom!

Concerning the erection of the Mashriqu'l-Adhkár: Now all the believers must become united, so that the temple may be built soon in one place. For should (the believers) undertake (the erection of a temple) in many places, it will not become completed anywhere; and as in Chicago they have preceded every other place to plan the erection of the temple, undoubtedly to co-operate and help them is noble and a necessity. Then when it is built in one place it will become erected in many other places. If, for the present you prepare or establish a home in New York, though by renting it, to become a center for the gathering of the believers in God, it is very acceptable. God willing in all the States of America in the future there will be erected temples with infinite architectural beauty, art, with pleasing proportion and handsome and attractive appearance.

* * * * *

O ye Friends of the Merciful:

I was delighted when my eyes beheld your illumined faces; My breast was thrilled with joy when I looked upon your faces and physical forms; My heart rejoiced on remembering your merciful attributes; My Spirit was cheered on pondering over the lofty gifts with which God has distinguished you by crowning you with crowns of the Kingdom in this glorious age and century from which brilliant lights will shine over all future ages and centuries.

Blessed are ye because of this favor which, like the brilliant Venus, the dazzling morning star, shines over all horizons.

119

Thank God that He hath chosen you from amongst the called souls, illumined your foreheads with this magnificent Light, made you enter this wide Gate, and informed you of the Manifestations of His Traces, and the source of His Mysteries.

Thank ye Him, for He hath appointed you signs of His Oneness, Standards of His Perfection, and lofty Trees in the garden of His Sanctity.

Be, therefore, in harmony and unison, in love and agreement; and bind yourselves with affinity upon all sides, that you may be as birds singing in the same garden - as fish swimming in the same sea - as lions roaring in the same thicket.

Though multiplied as waves in many forms, yet always the same sea raging and flowing, so be ye united in essence and spirit.

Be united and attracted to one purpose as moths are attracted to the light of the lamp.

This is that whereby your power is augmented; your loins strengthened; your words exalted; your trees fruitful; your gardens beautified; your basins flowing; your faces illumined, and your banners hoisted.

I supplicate God to continue to shower down upon you of His Holy abundance and His Merciful Revelations.

Verily He is the Almighty, the Protector, the Generous, the Giver and the Merciful

*(Received by New York Board of Council, August 2, 1902)*

120

# LETTER FROM SHOGHI EFFENDI

*Letter from Shoghi Effendi to the New York Spiritual Assembly:*

To the beloved of the Lord and the handmaids of the Merciful, throughout the City of New York, U.S.A. Care of the members of the Spiritual Assembly.

Dear and faithful friends of 'Abdu'l-Bahá!

The welcome letter which the members of your Spiritual Assembly have sent me is indeed a fresh and remarkable testimony of your wise, patient and persistent efforts to promote the Cause of God and deepen its foundations in the heart of that great city.

All throughout the various vicissitudes which the Movement has encountered during this past year of bereavement and uncertainty, the faithful lovers of the Master in New York have, by their wisdom in teaching, the range and character of their activities, their perseverance in their labors and their unity in service, proved themselves worthy of the blessings which our beloved 'Abdu'l-Bahá showered upon them during His repeated visits to their city. It is my earnest hope and prayer that now at this decisive hour of the Cause of God the friends may with clear vision and redoubled energy endeavor to deepen still further the essential truth of the Cause in their own lives, and then extend the sphere of their activity, endeavoring at all times to infuse the regenerating spirit of Bahá'u'lláh into the divers communities, creeds and classes that are represented in that most cosmopolitan city of the American continent.

From the leaflets, the circular letter and the pamphlet enclosed in the letter of your Spiritual Assembly, I can see clearly how well you have undertaken the task of acquainting the intellectual and religious circles of your city with the Divine Teachings, how admirably you have coordinated your efforts for service, and how beautifully

121

you have immortalized the memory of the Beloved's sojourn in your midst.

As I have already intimated in my first letter to the National Spiritual Assembly, I shall be most pleased to receive from every Bahá'í center throughout America regular and comprehensive reports on the position of the Cause and the activity of the friends. These I shall gladly transmit to the friends throughout the East, who in their present hour of restlessness and turmoil will, I am sure, be cheered to hear of the steady and peaceful growth of the Cause in your land. I have already shared the news you have conveyed to me with the resident friends in the Holy Land, and shall soon, by the aid of the Spiritual Assembly of Haifa, send them to the believers throughout the East.

Our departed Master, whose Call first awakened that city, who later visited it and with his own hands watered its soil, and who to his last hour bestowed his tenderest care upon it, is now, as ever before, watching from his Station on High the progress of the work which he has entrusted to you, his beloved children, ready to bless, guide and strengthen you in your efforts to achieve success for his Cause.

Awaiting your joyful news, and wishing you from all my heart the highest success in all your endeavors,

I am your devoted brother,

(signed) SHOGHI.

Haifa, Palestine, February 3, 1923.

# MAJOR ADDRESSES

## THE UNITY FEAST

*Unity Feast, June 29, 1912, at West Englewood, New Jersey.*

This event is commemorated every year with a picnic at the same location, now a Bahá'í property, on the last Saturday of June.

This is a delightful gathering; you have come here with sincere intentions and the purpose of all present is the attainment of the virtues of God. The motive is attraction to the divine Kingdom. Since the desire of all is unity and agreement it is certain that this meeting will be productive of great results. It will be the cause of attracting a new bounty, for we are turning to the Kingdom of Abhá seeking the infinite bestowals of the Lord. This is a new Day and this hour is a new Hour in which we have come together. Surely the Sun of Reality with its full effulgence will illumine us and the darkness of disagreements will disappear. The utmost love and unity will result, the favors of God will encompass us, the pathway of the Kingdom will be made easy. Like candles these souls will become ignited and made radiant through the lights of supreme guidance. Such gatherings as this have no equal or likeness in the world of mankind where people are drawn together by physical motives or in furtherance of material interests, for this meeting is a prototype of that inner and complete spiritual association in the eternal world of being.

True Bahá'í meetings are the mirrors of the Kingdom wherein images of the Supreme Concourse are reflected. In them the lights of the most great guidance are visible. They voice the summons of the heavenly Kingdom and echo the call of the angelic hosts to every listening ear. The efficacy of such meetings as these is permanent throughout the ages. This assembly has a name and significance which will last forever. Hundreds of thousands of meetings shall be held to commemorate this occasion and the very words I speak to you today shall be repeated in them for ages to come. Therefore be ye rejoiced for ye are sheltered beneath the providence of God. Be happy and joyous because the bestowals of God are intended for you and the life of the Holy Spirit is breathing upon you.

Rejoice, for the heavenly table is prepared for you.

Rejoice, for the angels of heaven are your assistants and helpers.

Rejoice, for the glance of the Blessed Beauty Bahá'u'lláh is directed upon you.

Rejoice, for Bahá'u'lláh is your protector.

Rejoice, for the glory everlasting is destined for you.

Rejoice, for the life eternal is awaiting you.

How many blessed souls have longed for this radiant century, their utmost hopes and desires centered upon the happiness and joy of one such day as this. Many the nights they passed sleepless and lamenting until the very morn in longing anticipation of this age, yearning to realize even an hour of this time. God has favored you in this century and has specialized you for the realization of its blessings. Therefore you must praise and thank God with heart and soul in appreciation of this great opportunity and the attainment of this infinite bestowal; that such doors have been opened before your faces, such abundance is pouring down from the cloud of mercy and that these refreshing breezes from the paradise of Abhá are resuscitating you. You must become of one heart, one spirit and one susceptibility. May you become as the waves of one sea, stars of the same heaven, fruits adorning the same tree, roses of one garden; in order that through you the oneness of humanity may establish its temple in the world of mankind, for you are the ones who are called to uplift the cause of unity among the nations of the earth.

First, you must become united and agreed among yourselves. You must be exceedingly kind and loving toward each other, willing to forfeit life in the pathway of another's happiness. You must be ready to sacrifice your possessions in another's behalf. The rich among you must show compassion toward the poor, and the well-to-do must look after those in distress. In Persia the friends offer their lives for each other, striving to assist and advance the interests and welfare of all the rest. They live in a perfect state of unity and agreement. Like the Persian friends you must be perfectly agreed and united to the extent and limit of sacrificing life. Your utmost desire must be to confer happiness upon each other. Each one must be the servant of the others, thoughtful of their comfort and welfare. In the path of God one must forget himself entirely. He must not consider his own pleasure but seek the pleasure of others. He must not desire glory nor gifts of bounty for himself but seek these gifts and blessings for his brothers and sisters. It is my hope that you may become like this; that you may attain to the supreme bestowal and be imbued with such spiritual qualities as to forget yourselves entirely and with heart and soul offer yourselves as sacrifices for the Blessed Perfection. You should have neither will nor desire of your own but seek everything for the beloved of God and live together in complete love and fellowship. May the favors of Bahá'u'lláh surround you from all directions. This is the greatest bestowal and supreme bounty. These are the infinite favors of God.

# 'ABDU'L-BAHÁ'S FIRST PUBLIC ADDRESS IN THE UNITED STATES

*Address delivered by 'Abdu'l-Bahá at the Church of the Ascension, 5th Avenue and Tenth Street on April 14, 1912.*

A second address was delivered by 'Abdu'l-Bahá at the Church of the Ascension on June 2, 1912 at the People Forum.

In his scriptural lesson this morning the revered Doctor read a verse from the Epistle of St. Paul to the Corinthians: "For now we see through a glass darkly, but then face to face."

The light of truth has heretofore been seen dimly through variegated glasses, but now the splendors of divinity shall be visible through the translucent mirrors of pure hearts and spirits. The light of truth is the divine teaching, heavenly instruction, merciful principles and spiritual civilization. Since my arrival in this country I find that material civilization has progressed greatly; that commerce has attained the utmost degree of expansion; arts, agriculture and all details of material civilization have reached the highest stage of perfection; but spiritual civilization has been left behind. Material civilization is like unto the lamp, while spiritual civilization is the light in that lamp. If the material and spiritual civilization become united, then we will have the light and the lamp together and the outcome will be perfect. For material civilization is like unto a beautiful body and spiritual civilization is like unto the spirit of life. If that wondrous spirit of life enters this beautiful body, the body will become a channel for the distribution and development of the perfections of humanity.

His Holiness Jesus Christ came to teach the people of the world this heavenly civilization and not material civilization. He breathed the breath of the Holy Spirit into the body of the world and established an illumined civilization. Among the principles of divine civilization he came to proclaim is the "Most Great Peace" of mankind. Among his principles of spiritual civilization is the oneness of the kingdom of humanity. Among the principles of heavenly civilization he brought is the virtue of the human world. Among the principles of celestial civilization he announced is the improvement and betterment of human morals.

Today the world of humanity is in need of international unity and conciliation. To establish these great fundamental principles a propelling power is needed. It is self-evident that unity of the human world and the "Most Great Peace" cannot be accomplished through material means. They cannot be established through political power, for the political interests of nations are various and the policies of peoples are divergent and conflicting. They cannot be founded through racial or patriotic power, for these are human powers, selfish and weak. The very nature of racial differences and patriotic prejudices prevents the realization of this unity and agreement. Therefore it is evidenced that the promotion of the oneness of the kingdom of humanity which is the essence of the teachings of all the manifestations of God is impossible except through the divine power and breaths of the Holy Spirit. Other powers are too weak and are incapable of accomplishing this.

For man, two wings are necessary. One wing is physical power and material civilization; the other is spiritual power and divine civilization. With one wing only, flight is impossible. Two wings are essential. Therefore no matter how much material civilization advances it cannot attain to perfection except through uplift of the spiritual civilization.

All the prophets have come to promote divine bestowals, to found the spiritual civilization and teach the principles of morality. Therefore we must strive with all our powers so that spiritual influences may gain the victory. For material forces have attacked mankind. The world of humanity is submerged in a sea of materialism. The rays of the Sun of Reality are seen but dimly and darkly through

128

opaque glasses. The penetrative power of the divine bounty is not fully manifest.

In Persia, among the various religions and sects there were intense differences. His Holiness Bahá'u'lláh appeared in that country and founded the spiritual civilization. He established affiliation among the various peoples, promoted the oneness of the human world and unfurled the banner of the "Most Great Peace." He wrote special epistles covering these facts to all the kings and rulers of nations. Sixty years ago he conveyed his message to the leaders of the political world and to high dignitaries of the spiritual world. Therefore spiritual civilization is progressing in the Orient and oneness of humanity and peace among the nations is being accomplished step by step. Now I find a strong movement for Universal Peace emanating from America. It is my hope that this standard of the oneness of the world of humanity may be upraised with the utmost solidity, so that the Orient and Occident may become perfectly reconciled, attain complete inter-communication, the hearts of the East and West become united and attracted, real union become unveiled, the light of guidance shine, divine effulgences be seen day by day so that the world of humanity may find complete tranquility, the eternal happiness of man become evident and the hearts of the people of the world be as mirrors in which the rays of the Sun of Reality may be reflected. Consequently it is my request that you should strive so that the light of reality may shine and the everlasting felicity of the world of man become apparent.

I will pray for you so you may attain this everlasting happiness. When I arrived in this city I was made very happy for I perceived that the people here have capacity for divine bestowals and have worthiness for the civilization of heaven. I pray that you may attain to all merciful bounties.

Prayer:

O Almighty! O God! O Thou compassionate One! This servant of thine has hastened to the regions of the west from the uttermost parts of the east that perchance these nostrils may be perfumed by the fragrances of thy bestowals; that the breeze of the rose-garden of guidance may blow over these cities; that the people may attain to the capacity of receiving thy favors; that the hearts may be rejoiced through thy glad-tidings; that the eyes may behold the light of reality; that the ears may hearken to the call of the kingdom. O Almighty! Illumine the hearts. O kind God! Make the souls the envy of the rose-garden and the meadow. O incomparable beloved! Waft the fragrance of thy bounty. Radiate the lights of compassion so that the hearts may be cleansed and purified and that they may take a share and portion from thy confirmations. Verily this congregation is seeking thy path, searching for thy mystery, beholding thy face and desiring to be characterized with thine attributes.

O Almighty! Confer Thy infinite bounties. Bestow Thy inexhaustible treasury so that these impotent ones may become powerful.

Verily thou art the kind! Thou art the generous! Thou art the omniscient, the omnipotent!

# FIRST ADDRESS ON RACE UNITY

*Talk Given by 'Abdul-Bahá at 780 West End Avenue, New York City (Home of Mr. and Mrs. E. B. Kinney), April 17, 1912.*

In the Holy Books it is recorded that when the Sun of Truth dawns it will appear in the East and its Light will be reflected in the West. Already its dawning has taken place in the East and its signs are appearing in the West. Its illumination shall spread rapidly and widely in the Occident. That Sun of Truth has risen in Persia and its effulgence is now manifest here in America. This is the greatest proof of its appearance in the horizon of the world, as recorded in the Heavenly Books. Praise be to God! that which is prophesied in the Holy Books has been fulfilled.

On Sunday last, at Carnegie Hall, the revered soul who introduced 'Abdu'l-Bahá gave voice to the statement that according to tradition demons would appear from the land of the sun-rising, but now we find angels appearing instead. At the time this statement was made a reply was not possible but today we will speak of it. The great Spiritual Lights have appeared only in the East. The Blessed Perfection Bahá'u'lláh appeared in the East. His Holiness Jesus Christ dawned on the horizon of the East. Moses, Aaron, Joseph and all the Israelite prophets such as Jeremiah, Ezekiel, Isaiah and others, appeared from the Orient. The Lights of Mohammed and the Báb shone from the East. The Eastern horizon has been flooded with the effulgence of these great lights, and only from the East have they risen to shine upon the West. Now, praise be to God! you are living in the dawn of a cycle when the Sun of Truth is again shining forth from the East, illumining all regions.

The world has become a new world. The darkness of night which has enveloped humanity is passing. A new day has dawned. Divine susceptibilities and heavenly capacities are developing in human souls under the training of the Sun of Truth. The capacities of souls are different. Their conditions are various. For example, certain minerals come from the stony regions of the earth. All are minerals; all are produced by the same sun, but one remains a stone while another develops the capacity of a glittering gem or jewel. From one plot of land tulips and hyacinths grow; from another, thorns and thistles. Each plot receives the bounty of the sunshine, but the capacity to receive it is not the same. Therefore it is requisite that we must develop capacity and Divine susceptibility in order that the merciful Bounty of the Sun of Truth intended for this age and time in which we are living, may reflect from us as light from pure crystals.

The Bounties of the Blessed Perfection are infinite. We must endeavor to increase our capacity daily, to strengthen and enlarge our capabilities for receiving them; become as perfect mirrors. The more polished and clean the mirror, the more effulgent is its reflection of the Lights of the Sun of Truth. Be like a well cultivated garden wherein the roses and variegated flowers of heaven are growing in fragrance and beauty. It is my hope that your hearts may become as ready ground, carefully tilled and prepared, upon which the Divine showers of the Bounties of the Blessed Perfection may descend and the zephyrs of this Divine springtime may blow with quickening breath. Then will the garden of your hearts bring forth its flowers of delightful fragrance to refresh the nostril of the Heavenly Gardener. Let your hearts reflect the glories of the Sun of Truth in their many colors to gladden the eye of the Divine Cultivator who has nourished them. Day by day become more closely attracted in order that the Love of God may illumine all those with whom you come in contact. Be as one spirit, one soul, leaves of one tree, flowers of one garden, waves of one ocean.

As difference in degree of capacity exists among human souls; as difference in capability is found, therefore individuals will differ one from another. But in reality this is a cause of unity and not of discord and enmity. If the flowers of a garden were all of one color, the effect would be monotonous to the eye; but if the colors are variegated, it is most pleasing and wonderful. The difference in adornment of color and capacity of reflection among the flowers gives the garden its beauty and charm. Therefore, although we are of different individualities, different in ideas, and of various fragrances, let us strive like flowers of the same Divine garden to live together in harmony. Even though each soul has its own individual perfume and color, all are reflecting the same Light, all contributing fragrance to the same breeze which blows through the garden, all continuing to grow in complete harmony and accord. Become as waves of one sea; trees of one forest, growing in the utmost love, agreement and unity.

If you attain to such a capacity of love and unity, the Blessed Perfection will shower infinite graces of the Spiritual Kingdom upon you, guide, protect and preserve you under the shadow of His Word, increase your happiness in this world and uphold you through all difficulties. Therefore it is my hope that day by day you will become more and more effulgent in the horizon of Heaven, advance nearer and nearer toward the Kingdom of El-Abhá, attain greater and greater bounties of the Blessed Perfection. I am joyful, for I perceive the evidences of great love among you. I go to Chicago, and when I return I hope that love will have become infinite. Then will it be an eternal joy to me and the friends in the Orient.

# RELIGION & SCIENCE

*Address of 'Abdu'l-Bahá at Earl Hall, Columbia University,
New York, April 19, 1912.*

If an observing man looks around him in the world of creation, he will find that created things are divisible into three classes. First: created things of the mineral type; that is to say, matter or substance which has taken various forms and shapes. The second kind of created phenomena are the plants or vegetable kingdom. The vegetable possesses the virtues of the mineral plus the power or virtue of change; that is to say, the power of growth. Hence plant life is a step further and more specialized than the mineral. The third created object is the animal. The animal possesses the virtues of the mineral and the virtues of the vegetable, but above that, it is endowed with sensation. It has the sense of sight, hearing, taste, smell and touch. Therefore the animal is possessed of the virtues of the mineral, the vegetable and in addition is endowed with peculiar qualities of sensitiveness. But man who is the most specialized form of creation embodies all the virtues of the mineral, vegetable and animal, plus an ideal power which is not to be found in the others, which is absolutely absent in the others. This can be said to be the power of intellect. The outcome of this intellectual power is science, which is especially characteristic of man. This is the power of external investigation, the discoverer of the mysteries of outer phenomena. This scientific power comprehends all created objects. This power verily can discover the hidden and mysterious things of the earth. In man alone this is noticeable. The most noble virtue, the most praiseworthy accomplishment of man therefore is scientific attainment.

Science may be likened to a mirror wherein are reflected the images of these mysteries of outer phenomena. It brings forth and exhibits to us in the arena of knowledge all the products of the past. It links together past and present The philosophical conclusions of bygone centuries, the teaching of the prophets and wisdom of former sages are crystallized and reproduced in the scientific advancements of today. Science is the discoverer of the past. From its premises of past and present we deduce conclusions as to the future. Science is the governor of nature and its mysteries, the one agency by which man explores the institutions of material creation. All created things are captive of nature and subject to its laws. They cannot transgress the control of these laws in one detail or particular. The infinite starry worlds and heavenly bodies are nature obedient subjects. The earth and its myriad organisms, all minerals, plants and animals are thralls of its dominion. But man through the exercise of his scientific, intellectual power can rise out of this condition, can modify, change and control nature according to his own wishes and uses. Science, so to speak, is the breaker of the laws of nature.

Consider, for example, man, according to natural law, should dwell upon the earth. But breaking this law he can sail in vessels over the ocean, fly in the atmosphere in airships or advance through the depths of the sea in submarines. This is against the law of nature; this breaks the sovereignty of nature. According to nature's laws and methods all the science we have, all the inventions and discoveries we have should be hidden. According to nature they should not be open and known, they should be mysteries. But man through the power of science takes them out of the plane of the invisible and unknown, breaks the very laws of nature, draws them into the plane of the visible, exposes and explains them. For instance one of the mysteries of nature is electricity. According to nature this force, this energy should be latent and hidden, but man through his scientific power breaks the laws of nature, arrests it and even imprisons it for his use.

In short, man through this scientific power is the most noble product of creation, the governor of nature. He takes the sword from nature's hand and uses it on nature's head. According to nature the night is to be dark and gloomy but man takes his sword of electricity, this electric sword, kills the darkness and dispels the gloom. Man is progressive, nature is not; man has memory, nature has not. Man is a sensitive being, nature is minus. Man is nobler than nature. There are certain powers in man which are absent in nature. If it be claimed that these powers which are present in man are from nature itself, that man is a part of nature, in response to this we will say that if nature is the whole and man is part of that whole, the question arises is it possible for a part to possess virtues which are absent in the whole? No, undoubtedly the part must be endowed with the same qualities and properties as the whole. For example, the hair is a part of this human anatomy. It cannot contain elements which are absent in other parts of the body, for in all cases the elements composing the body are the same. Therefore it becomes evident and manifest that man although in body a part of nature, nevertheless in spirit possesses a power which is beyond nature; because were he simply a part of nature he could possess only the things which nature possesses. God has conferred upon and added to man this distinctive power, this power of intellect, this power or faculty of knowledge; and its greatest virtue is scientific enlightenment.

Inasmuch as this is an endowment for the acquisition of knowledge it is therefore the most praiseworthy power of all, for by it and through its attainments the betterment of the human race is accomplished, the development of human virtues is made possible and the spirit and mysteries of God become manifest. Therefore I am very pleased with my visit to this university. Praise be to God, that this country abounds in such institutions of learning where all the sciences and arts may easily be acquired.

Just as material and physical sciences may be acquired here and are constantly unfolding in wider vistas of attainment, I am hopeful that spiritual development also may keep pace with these outer advantages. As material knowledge is illuminating those within the walls of this temple of learning, so also may the light of the spirit, the inner and spiritual light of the real philosophy illuminate this institution. The most important principle of divine philosophy is the oneness of the world of humanity, the unity of mankind, the bond conjoining the East and the West, the tie of love which should bind the hearts of men.

Therefore it is our duty to put forth our greatest efforts and summon our energies from all directions in order that the bonds of unity and accord may be established among mankind. For six thousand years we have had bloodshed and strife. It is enough; it is sufficient. Now is the time to associate together in love and harmony. For six thousand years we have tried the sword and warfare; let mankind for a time at least live in peace. Review history and consider how much savagery, how much bloodshed and warfare the world has witnessed. It has been either religious warfare, political warfare or some clash of human interests. The world of humanity has not enjoyed peace even for a single day. Year by year the implements of warfare have been increased and perfected. Consider the past centuries; when war took place only ten, fifteen, or twenty thousand at the most were killed, but now it is possible to kill one hundred thousand in a single day. Then warfare was carried on with the sword; today it is the smokeless gun. Formerly battleships consisted of sailing vessels; today there are dreadnoughts. Consider the increase and improvement in the implements of warfare. God has created us all human, and all countries of the earth are parts of the same globe. We are all servants of Him. He is kind and just to all. Why should we be unkind and unjust to each other? He provides for all. Why should we deprive one another? He protects and preserves all. Why should we kill our fellow-creatures? If this warfare and strife be for the sake of religion, religion has no part in it. All the Divine Manifestations have promulgated the Oneness of God and the unity of Mankind. They have taught that men should love and mutually help each other in order that they might progress. Now if this conception of religion be true, its essential principle is the oneness of humanity. The fundamental truth of the Manifestations is peace. This fundamental truth underlies all religion, all justice. The Divine purpose is that men should live in unity, concord and agreement and should love one another. Consider the virtues of the human world and realize that the oneness of humanity is the primary foundation of them all. Read the Gospel and the other Holy

Books. You will find their fundamentals are one and the same. Therefore unity is the essential truth of Religion, and when so understood embraces all the virtues of the human world. Praise be to God, this knowledge has been spread, eyes have been opened and ears have become attentive. Therefore we must endeavor to promulgate and practice the Religion of God which has been founded by all the Prophets. And the Religion of God in short is absolute love and unity.

# THE MOST GREAT PEACE

*Reception by the New York Peace Society,*
*Hotel Astor, May 13, 1912.*

Today there is no greater glory for man than that of service in the cause of the "Most Great Peace." Peace is light whereas war is darkness. Peace is life; war is death. Peace is guidance; war is error. Peace is the foundation of God; war is a satanic institution. Peace is the illumination of the world of humanity; war is the destroyer of human foundations. When we consider outcomes in the world of existence we find that peace and fellowship are factors of upbuilding and betterment whereas war and strife are the causes of destruction and disintegration. All created things are expressions of the affinity and cohesion of elementary substances, and non-existence is the absence of their attraction and agreement. Various elements unite harmoniously in composition but when these elements become discordant, repelling each other, decomposition and non-existence result. Everything partakes of this nature and is subject to this principle, for the creative foundation in all its degrees and kingdom is an expression or outcome of love. Consider the restlessness and agitation of the human world today because of war. Peace is health and construction; war is disease and dissolution. When the banner of truth is raised, peace becomes the cause of the welfare and advancement of the human world. In all cycles and ages war has been a factor of derangement and discomfort whereas peace and brotherhood have brought security and consideration to human interests. This distinction is especially pronounced in the present world conditions, for warfare in former centuries had not attained the degree of savagery and destructiveness which now characterizes it. If two nations were at war in olden times, ten or twenty thousand would be sacrificed but in this century the destruction of one hundred thousand lives in a day is quite possible. So perfected has the science of killing become and so efficient the means and instruments of its accomplishment that a whole nation can be obliterated in a short time. Therefore comparison with the methods and results of ancient warfare is out of the question.

According to an intrinsic law, all phenomena of being attain to a summit and degree of consummation, after which a new order and condition is established. As the instruments and science of war have reached the degree of thoroughness and proficiency, it is hoped that the transformation of the human world is at hand and that in the coming centuries all the energies and inventions of man will be utilized in promoting the interest of peace and brotherhood. Therefore may this esteemed and worthy society for the establishment of international peace be confirmed in its sincere intentions and empowered by God. Then will it hasten the time when the banner of universal agreement will be raised and international welfare will be proclaimed and consummated so that the darkness which now encompasses the world shall pass away.

Sixty years ago His Holiness Bahá'u'lláh was in Persia. Seventy years ago His Holiness the Báb appeared there. These two blessed souls devoted their lives to the foundation of international peace and love among mankind. They strove with heart and soul to establish the teachings by which divergent people might be brought together and no strife, rancor or hatred prevail. His Holiness Bahá'u'lláh, addressing all humanity, said that Adam the parent of mankind may be likened to the tree of nativity upon which you are the leaves and blossom. Inasmuch as your origin was one, you must now be united and agreed; you must consort with each other in joy and fragrance. He pronounced prejudice, whether religious, racial, patriotic, political, the destroyer of the body politic. He said that man must recognize the oneness of humanity, for all in origin belong to the same household and all are servants of the same God. Therefore mankind must continue in the state of fellowship and love, emulating the institutions of God and turning away from satanic promptings, for the divine bestowals bring forth unity and agreement whereas satanic readings induce hatred and war.

This remarkable Personage was able by these principles to establish a bond of unity among the differing sects and divergent people of Persia. Those who followed his teachings, no matter from what denomination or faction they came, were conjoined by the ties of love, until now they co-operate and live together in peace and agreement. They are real brothers and sisters. No distinctions of class are observed among them and complete harmony prevails. Daily this bond of affinity is strengthening and their spiritual fellowship continually develops. In order to insure the progress of mankind and to establish these principles His Holiness Bahá'u'lláh suffered every ordeal and difficulty. His Holiness the Báb became a martyr, and over twenty thousand men and women sacrificed their lives for their faith. His Holiness Bahá'u'lláh was imprisoned and subjected to severe persecutions. Finally he was exiled from Persia to Mesopotamia; from Baghdad he was sent to Constantinople and Adrianople and from thence to the prison of 'Akká in Syria. Through all these ordeals he strove day and night to proclaim the oneness of humanity and promulgate the message of Universal Peace. From the prison of 'Akká he addressed the kings and rulers of the earth in lengthy letters summoning them to international agreement and explicitly stating that the standard of the "Most Great Peace" would surely be upraised in the world.

This has come to pass. The powers of earth cannot withstand the privileges and bestowals which God has ordained for this great and glorious century. It is a need and exigency of the time. Man can withstand anything except that which is divinely intended and indicated for the age and its requirements. Now, praise be to God! in all countries of the world, lovers of peace are to be found and these principles are being spread among mankind, especially in this country. Praise be to God! this thought is prevailing and souls are continually arising as defenders of the oneness of humanity, endeavoring to assist and establish international peace.

There is no doubt that this wonderful democracy will be able to realize it, and the banner of international agreement will be unfurled here to spread onward and outward among all the nations of the world. I give thanks to God that I find you imbued with such susceptibilities and lofty aspirations, and I hope that you will be the means of spreading this light to all men. Thus may the Sun of Reality shine upon the East and the West. The enveloping clouds shall pass away, and the heat of the divine rays will dispel the mist. The reality of man shall develop and come forth as the image of God, his Creator. The thoughts of man shall take such upward flight that former accomplishments shall appear as the play of children, for the ideas and beliefs of the past and the prejudices regarding race and religion have ever lowered and been destructive to human evolution. I am most hopeful that in this century these lofty thoughts shall be conductive to human welfare.

Let this century be the sun of previous centuries the effulgences of which shall last forever, so that in times to come they shall glorify the twentieth century, saying the twentieth century was the century of light, the twentieth century was the century of life, the twentieth century was the century of international peace, the twentieth century was the century of divine bestowals and the twentieth century has left traces which shall last forever.

# THE EQUALITY OF WOMAN AND MAN

*'Abdu'l-Bahá addresses a Woman's Suffrage Meeting,*
*Metropolitan Temple, Seventh Avenue and Fourteenth Street,*
*New York, May 20, 1912.*

Today questions of the utmost importance are facing humanity, questions peculiar to this radiant century. In former centuries there was not even mention of them. Inasmuch as this is the century of illumination, the century of humanity, the century of divine bestowals. These questions are being presented for the expression of public opinion, and in all the countries of the world, discussion is taking place looking to their solution.

One of these questions concerns the rights of woman and her equality with man. In past ages it was held that woman and man were not equal – that is to say, woman was considered inferior to man, even from the standpoint of her anatomy and creation. She was considered especially inferior in intelligence, and the idea prevailed universally that it was not allowable for her to step into the arena of important affairs. In some countries man went so far as to believe and teach that woman belonged to a sphere lower than human. But in this century, which is the century of light and the revelation of mysteries, God is proving to the satisfaction of humanity that all this is ignorance and error; nay, rather, it is well established that mankind and womankind as parts of composite humanity are coequal and that no difference in estimate is allowable, for all are human. The conditions in past centuries were due to woman's lack of opportunity. She was denied the right and privilege of education and left in her undeveloped state. Naturally, she could not and did not advance. In reality, God has created all mankind. And in the estimation of God there is no distinction as to male and female. The one whose heart is pure is acceptable in His sight, be that one man or woman. God does not inquire, "Art thou woman or art thou man?" He judges human action. If these are acceptable in the threshold of the Glorious One, man and woman will be equally recognized and rewarded.

Furthermore, the education of woman is more necessary and important that of man, for woman is the trainer of the child from its infancy. If she be defective and imperfect herself, the child will necessarily be deficient, therefore, imperfection of woman implies a condition of imperfection in all mankind, for it is the mother who rears, nurtures and guides the growth of the child. This is not the function of the father. If the educator is incompetent, the educated will be correspondingly lacking. This is evident and incontrovertible. Could the student be brilliant and accomplished if the teacher is illiterate and ignorant? The mothers are the first educators of mankind; if they be imperfect, alas for the condition and future of the race.

Again, it is well established in history that where woman has not participated in human affairs the outcomes have never attained a state of completion and perfection. On the other hand, every influential undertaking of the human world wherein woman has been a participant has attained importance. This is historically true and beyond disproof even in religion. Jesus Christ had twelve disciples and among His followers a woman known as Mary Magdalene. Judas Iscariot has become a traitor and hypocrite, and after the crucifixion the remaining eleven disciples were wavering and undecided, It is certain from the evidence of the Gospels that the one who comforted them and reestablished their faith was Mary Magdalene.

The world of humanity consists of two parts, male and female. Each is the complement of the other. Therefore, if one is defective, the other will necessarily be incomplete, and perfection cannot be attained. There is a right hand and a left hand in the human body, functionally equal in service and administration. If either proves defective, the defect will naturally extend to the other by involving the completeness of the whole; for accomplishment is not normal unless both are perfect. If we say one hand is deficient, we prove the inability and incapacity of the other; for single-handed there is no full

144

accomplishment. Just as physical accomplishment is complete with two hands, so man and woman, the two parts of the social body, must be perfect. It is not natural that either should remain undeveloped, and until both are perfected, the happiness of the human world will not be realized.

The most momentous question of this day is international peace and arbitration, and universal peace is impossible without universal suffrage. Children are educated by the women. The mother bears the troubles and anxieties of rearing the child, undergoes the ordeal of its birth and training. Therefore, it is more difficult for mothers to send to the battlefield those upon whom they have lavished such love and care. Consider a son reared and trained twenty years by a devoted mother. What sleepless nights and restless, anxious days she has spent! Having brought him through dangers and difficulties to the age of maturity, how agonizing then to sacrifice him upon the battlefield! Therefore, the mothers will not sanction war nor be satisfied with it. So it will come to pass that when women participate fully and equally in the affairs of the world, when they enter confidently and capably the great arena of laws and politics, war will cease; for woman will be the obstacle and hindrance to it. This is true and without doubt.

It has been objected by some that woman is not equally capable with man and that she is deficient by creation. This is pure imagination. The difference in capability between man and woman is due entirely to opportunity and education. Heretofore woman has been denied the right and privilege of equal development. If equal opportunity is granted her, there is no doubt she will be the peer of man. History will evidence this. In past ages noted women have arisen in the affairs of nations and surpassed men in their accomplishments. Among them was Zenobia, Queen of the East, whose capital was Palmyra. Even today the site of that city bears witness to her greatness, ability and sovereignty; for there the traveler will find ruins of palaces and fortifications of the utmost strength and solidity built by this remarkable woman in the third century after Christ. She was the wife of the governor-general of Athens.

After her husband's death she assumed control of the government in his stead and rules her province most efficiently. Afterward, she conquered Syria, subdued Egypt and founded a most wonderful kingdom with political sagacity and thoroughness. The Roman Empire sent a great army against her. When this army replete with martial splendor reached Syria, Zenobia herself appeared upon the field leading her forces. On the day of battle she arrayed herself in regal garments, placed a crown upon her head and rode forth, sword in hand, to meet the invading legions. By her courage and military strategy the Roman army was routed and so completely dispersed that they were not able to reorganize in retreat. The government of Rome held consultation saying, "No matter what commander we send, we cannot overcome her; therefore, the Emperor Aurelian himself must go to lead the legions of Rome against Zenobia." Aurelian marched into Syria with two hundred thousands soldiers. The army of Zenobia was greatly inferior in size. The Romans besieged her in Palmyra two years without success. Finally, Aurelian was able to cut off the city's supplies of provisions so that she and her people were compelled by starvation to surrender. She was not defeated in battle. Aurelian carried her captive to Rome. On the day of his entry into the city he arranged a triumphal procession – first, elephants, then lions, tigers, birds. Monkeys – and after the monkeys, Zenobia. A crown was upon her head, a chain of gold about her neck. With queenly dignity and unconscious of humiliation, looking to the right and the left, she said: "Verily, I glory in being a woman and in having withstood the Roman Empire." (At that time the dominion of Rome covered half the known earth) "And this chain about my neck is a sign not of humiliation but of glorification. This is a symbol of my power not of my defeat."

Among other historical women was Catherine I, wife of Peter the Great. Russia and Turkey were at war. Muhammad Páshá commander of the Turkish forces, had defeated Peter and was about to take St. Petersburg. The Russian were in a most critical position. Catherine, the wife of Peter, said, "I will arrange this matter." She had an interview with Muhammad Páshá, negotiated a treaty of peace and induced him to turn back. She saved her husband and her nation. This was a great accomplishment. Afterward she was crowned Empress of Russia and ruled with wisdom until her death.

The discovery of America by Columbus was during the reign of Isabella of Spain, to whose intelligence and assistance this wonderful accomplishment was largely due. In brief, many remarkable women have appeared in the history of the world, but further mention of them is not necessary.

Today among the Bahá'ís of Persia there are many women who are the very pride and envy of the men. They are imbued with all the virtues and excellence of humanity. They are eloquent; they are poets and scholars and embody the quintessence of humility. In political ability and acumen they have been able to cope and compete with representative men. They have consecrated their lives and forfeited their possessions in martyrdom for the sake of humanity, and the traces of their glory will last forever. The pages of the history of Persia are illuminated by the lives and records of these women.

The purpose, in brief, is this: that if woman is fully educated and granted her rights, she will attain the capacity for wonderful accomplishments and prove herself the equal of man. She is the coadjutor of man, his complement and helpmeet. Both are human; both are endowed with potentialities of intelligence and embody the virtues of humanity. In all human powers and functions they are partners and coequals. At present in spheres of human activity woman does not manifest her natal prerogatives, owing to lack of education and opportunity. Without doubt education will establish her equality with man. Consider the animal kingdom, where no distinction is observed between male and female. They are equal in powers and privileges. Among birds of the air no distinction is evidenced. Their powers are equal, they dwell together in complete unity and mutual recognition of rights. Shall we not enjoy the same equality? Its absence is not befitting to mankind.

# THE ETERNAL CREATION

*'Abdu'l-Bahá talks in His home, 309 West*
*Seventy- Eighth Street, New York, July 5, 1912.*

Question: You have stated that we are living in a universal cycle, the first Manifestation of which was Adam and the manifestation of which is Bahá'u'lláh. Does this imply that other universal cycles preceded this one and that all traces of them have been effaced – cycles in which the ultimate purpose was the divine spiritualization of man just as it is the creative intention in this one?

The divine sovereignty is an ancient sovereignty, not an accidental sovereignty.

If we imagine this world of existence has a beginning, we can say the divine sovereignty is accidental – that is, there was a time when it did not exist. A king without a kingdom is impossible. He cannot be without a country, without subjects, without an army, without dominion, or he will be without kingship. All these exigencies or requirements of sovereignty must exist for a king. When they do exist, we can apply the word sovereignty to him. Otherwise, his sovereignty is imperfect, incomplete. If none of these conditions exists, sovereignty does not exist.

If we acknowledge that there is a beginning for this world of creation, we acknowledge that the sovereignty of God is accidental – that is, we admit a time when the reality of Divinity has been without dominion (lit. "defeated"). The names and attributes of Divinity are requirements of this world. The names the Powerful, the Living, the Provider. The Creator require and necessitate the existence of creatures. If there were no creatures, Creator would be meaningless. If there were none to provide for, we could not think of the Provider. If there were no life, the Living will be beyond the power of

148

conception. Therefore, all the names and attributes of God require the existence of objects or creatures upon which they have been bestowed and in which they have become manifest. If there was a time when no creation existed, when there was none to provide for, it would imply a time when there was no existent One, no Trainer and the attributes and qualities of God would have been meaningless and without significance. Therefore, the requirements of the attributes of God do not admit of cessation or interruption, for the names of God are actually and forever existing and not potential. Because they convey life, they are called Life-giving, because they provide, they are called Bountiful, the Provider, because they create, they are called Creator; because they educate and govern, the name Lord God is applied. That is to say, the divine names emanate from the eternal attributes of Divinity. Therefore, it is proved that the divine names presuppose the existence of objects or beings.

How then is a time conceivable when this sovereignty has not been existent? This divine sovereignty is not to be measured by six thousand years. This interminable, illimitable universe is not the result of that measured period. This stupendous laboratory and workshop has not been limited in its production to six thousand revolutions of the earth about the sun. With the slighted reflection man can be assured that this calculation and announcement is childish, especially in view of the fact that it is scientifically proved the terrestrial globe has been the habitation of man long prior to such a limited estimate.

As to the record in the Bible concerning Adam's entering paradise, His eating from the tree and His expulsion through the temptation of Satan: These are all symbols beneath which there are wonderful and divine meanings not to be calculated in years, dates and measurement of time. Likewise, the statement that God created the heaven and the earth in six days is symbolic. We will not explain this further today. The texts of the Holy Book are all symbolical, needing authoritative interpretation.

When man casts even a cursory glance of reflection upon the question of the universe, he discovers it is very ancient. A Persian philosopher was looking up into the heavens, lost in wonder, He said,

"I have written a book containing seventy proofs of the accidental appearance of the universe, but I still find it very ancient."

Bahá'u'lláh says: "The universe hath neither beginning nor ending." He has set aside the elaborate theories and exhaustive opinions of scientists and material philosophers by the simple statement, "There is no beginning, no ending." The theologians and religionists advance plausible proofs that the creation of the universe dates back six thousand years; the scientists bring forth indisputable facts and say, "No! These evidences indicate ten, twenty, fifty thousand years ago," etc. There are endless discussions pro and con. Bahá'u'lláh sets aside these discussions by one word and statement. He says, "The divine sovereignty hath no beginning and no ending." By this announcement and its demonstration He has established a standard of agreement among those who reflect upon this question of divine sovereignty; He has brought reconciliation and peace in this war of opinion and discussion.

Briefly, there were many cycles preceding this one in which we are living. They were consummated, completed and their traces obliterated. The divine and creative purpose in them was the evolution of spiritual man, just as it is in this cycle. The circle of existence is the same circle; it returns. The tree of life has ever borne the same heavenly fruit.

# BAHA'U'LLAH'S EPISTLES TO THE KINGS

*'Abdu'l-Bahá talks in His home, 309 West*
*Seventy-Eighth Street, New York, July 5, 1912.*

You are very welcome, very welcome, all of you! In the divine Holy Books there are unmistakable prophecies giving the glad tidings of a certain Day in which the Promised One of all the Books would appear, a radiant dispensation be established, the banner of the Most Great Peace and conciliation be hoisted and the oneness of the world of humanity proclaimed. Among the various nations and peoples of the world no enmity or hatred should remain. All hearts were to be connected one with another. These things are recorded in the Torah, or Old Testament, in the Gospels, the Qur'án, the Zend-Avesta, the books of Buddha and the book of Confucius. In brief, all the Holy Books contain these glad tidings. They announce that after the world is surrounded by darkness, radiance shall appear. For just as the night, when it becomes excessively dark, precedes the dawn of a new day, so likewise when the darkness of religious apathy and heedlessness overtakes the world, when human souls become negligent of God, when materialistic ideas overshadow spirituality, when nations become submerged in the world of matter and forget God – as such a time as this shall the divine Sun shine forth and the radiant morn appears.

Consider to what a remarkable extent the spirituality of people has been overcome by materialism so that spiritual susceptibility seems to have vanished, divine civilization become decadent, and guidance and knowledge of God no longer remain. All are submerged in the sea of materialism. Although some attend churches and temples of worship and devotion, it is in accordance with the traditions and imitations of their fathers and not for the investigation of reality. For it is evident they have not found reality and are not engaged in its adoration. They are holding to certain imitations which have descended to them from their fathers and ancestors. They have become accustomed to passing a certain length of time in temple worship and conforming to imitations and ceremonies. The proof of this is that the son of every Jewish father becomes a Jew and not a Christian; the son of every Muslim becomes a follower of Islam; the son of every Christian proves to be a Christian; the son of every Zoroastrian is a Zoroastrian, etc.

Therefore, religious faith and belief is merely a remnant of blind imitations which have descended through fathers and ancestors. Because this man's father was a Jew, he considers himself a Jew. Not that he has investigated reality and proved satisfactory to himself that Judaism is right – nay, rather, he is aware that his forefathers have followed this course; therefore, he had held to it himself.

The purpose of this is to explain that the darkness of imitations encompasses the world. Every nation is holding to its traditional religious forms. The light of reality is obscured. Were these various nations to investigate reality, there is no doubt they would attain to it. As reality is one, all nations would then become as one nation. So long as they adhere to various imitations and are deprived of reality, strife and warfare will continue and rancor and sedition prevail. If they investigate reality, never enmity nor rancor will remain, and they will attain to the utmost concord among themselves.

During the years when the darkness of heedlessness was most intense in the Orient and the people were so submerged in imitation that nations were thirsting for the blood of each other, considering each other as contaminated and refusing to associate – at such a time as this Bahá'u'lláh appeared. He arose in the Orient, uprooting the very foundations of imitations, and brought the dawn of the light of reality. Through Him various nations became united because all desired reality. Inasmuch as they investigated reality in religion, they found that all men are the servants of God, the posterity of Adam, children of one household and that the foundations of all the prophets are one. For inasmuch as the teaching of the Prophets are reality, Their foundation are one. The enmity and strife of nations, therefore, are due to religious imitations and not to reality which underlies the teachings of the Prophets. Through Bahá'u'lláh the nations and peoples grew to understand this. Therefore, hearts became united, and lives were cemented together. After centuries of hatred and bitterness the Christian, Jew, Zoroastrian, Muslin and Buddhist met in fellowship, all of them in the utmost love and unity. They became welded and cemented because they had perceived reality.

The divine Prophets are conjoined in the perfect state of love. Each One has given the glad tiding of His successor's coming and each successor has sanctioned the One Who precede Him. They were in the utmost unity but Their followers are in strife. For instance, Moses gave the message of the glad tiding of Christ, and Christ confirmed the Prophethood of Moses. Therefore between Moses and Jesus there is no variation or conflict. They are in perfect unity, but between the Jew and the Christian there is conflict. Now, therefore, if the Christian and the Jewish peoples investigate the reality underlying their Prophet's teachings, they will become kind in their attitude toward each other and associate in the utmost love, for reality is one and not dual or multiple. If this investigation of reality becomes universal, the divergent nations will ratify all the Divine Prophets and confirm all the Holy Books. No strife or rancor will then remain, and the world will become united. Then we will associate in the reality of love. We will become as fathers and sons, as brothers and sisters living together in complete unity, love and happiness; for this century is the century of light. It is not like former centuries. Former centuries were epochs of oppression. Now human intellects have developed, and human intelligence has increased. Each soul is investigating reality. This is not the time when we shall wage war and be hostile toward each other. We are living at a time when we should enjoy real friendship.

Fifty years ago Bahá'u'lláh sent Epistles to all the kings and nations of the world, at a time when there was no mention of international peace. One of these Epistles was sent by Him to the president of the American democracy. In these communications He summoned all to international peace and the oneness of the human world. He summoned mankind to the fundamentals of the teachings of all the Prophets. Some of the European kings were arrogant. Among them was Napoleon III. Bahá'u'lláh wrote a second Epistle to him, which was published thirty years ago. The context is this: O Napoleon! Thou hast become haughty indeed. Thou hast become proud. Thou hast forgotten God. Thou dost imagine that this majesty is permanent for thee, that this dominion is abiding for thee. A letter have we sent unto thee for acceptance with thy greatest love; but, instead, thou hast shown arrogance. Therefore God shall uproot the edifice of thy sovereignty; thy country shall flee away from thee. Thou shall find humiliation hastening after thee because thou didst not arise for that which was enjoined upon thee, whereas that which was a duty incumbent upon thee was the cause of life to the world. The punishment of God shall soon be dealt out to thee.

This Epistle was revealed in the year 1869, and after one year the foundation of the Napoleonic sovereignty was completely uprooted.

Among these Epistles was a very lengthy one to the Sháh of Persia. It was printed and spread broadcast throughout all the countries. This Epistle was revealed in the year 1870. In it Bahá'u'lláh admonished the Sháh of Persia to be kind to all his subjects, summoning him to dispense justice, counseling him to make no distinction between the religions, charging him to deal equally with Jew, Christian, Muslim and Zoroastrian and to remove the oppression prevailing in his country.

At that time, the Jews were greatly oppressed in Persia. Bahá'u'lláh especially recommended justice for them, saying that all people are the servants of God, and in the eyes of the government they should be equally estimated. "If justice is not dealt out, if these oppressions are not removed and if thou dost not obey God, the foundations of thy government will be razed, and thou shall become evanescent, become as nothing. Thou shouldst gather all the learned men, and then summon Me. There I shall be present. I will then advance proofs and evidences as of My validity. I will manifest My proof and anything that you may ask. I am ready. But if no attention is paid to this book, thou, like unto the kings who become nonexistent, shall likewise become nonexistent." The Sháh did not answer this Epistle of the Blessed Perfection. Then God destroyed the foundations of his sovereignty.

Among those to whom Bahá'u'lláh wrote was the Sultan of Turkey. In it He arraigned him, saying, "Verily, thou didst incarcerate and make Me a prisoner. Dost thou imagine that imprisonment is a loss to Me, that imprisonment is a humiliation for Me? This imprisonment is a glory for Me because it is in the pathway of God. I have not committed a crime. It is for the sake of God that I have received this ordeal. Therefore, I am very happy; I am exceedingly joyous. But thou must wait; God will send thee a punishment; thou shalt receive retribution. Erelong you shalt observe how ordeals shall descend upon thee like rain, and thou shalt become nonexistent." And even so it was.

Likewise, He sent messages to the other kings and crowned heads of the earth, summoning all of them to love, equity, international peace and the oneness of humanity in order that mankind might become unified and agreed; that strife, warfare and sedition should pass away; that bitterness and enmity might cease and all arise to serve the one God.

In brief, two kings arose against Bahá'u'lláh: the Sháh of Persia and the Sultan of Turkey. They imprisoned Him in the fortress of 'Akká in order to extinguished His light and exterminate His cause, but Bahá'u'lláh while in prison wrote severe letters of arraignment to them. He declared that imprisonment was no obstacle to Him. He said, "This imprisonment will prove to be the means of the promotion of My Cause. This imprisonment shall be the incentive for the spreading of My teachings. No harm shall come to Me because I have sacrificed My life, I have sacrificed My blood, I have sacrificed My possessions, I have sacrificed all and for Me this imprisonment is no loss." And just as He declared, so it came to pass. In prison He hoisted His banner, and His Cause spread throughout the world. It has reached America. Now the Cause of Bahá'u'lláh is extending to all nations of the world. You go to Asia, and wherever you travel you will find Bahá'ís. You go to Africa, Europe; there you will find the Cause of Bahá'u'lláh. In America it is just beginning to grow and spread.

These two kings could not do anything to withstand Bahá'u'lláh, but God through Him was capable to destroy both of them. I, too, was in prison. God removes the chains from my neck and placed them around the neck of 'Abdu'l-Hamíd. It was done suddenly – not in a long time. In a moment as it were. The same hour that the Young Turks declared liberty, the Committee of Union and Progress set me free. They lifted the chains from my neck  and threw them around the neck of "Abdu'l-Hamíd. That which he did to me was inflicted upon him. Now the position is precisely reversed. His days are spent in prison just as I passed the days in prison at 'Akká, with this difference: that I was happy in imprisonment. I was in the utmost elation because I was not a criminal. They had imprisoned me in the path of God. Every time I thought of this, that I was a prisoner in the pathway of God, the utmost elation overcame me. 'Abdu'l-Hamíd is now suffering punishment for his deeds. Because of the sins he committed, he is now in prison. This is retribution for the acts. Every hour he is mortified anew and he ignominy revived. He is in the utmost sorrow and disappointment while I am in perfect happiness. I was happy that – praise to God! - I was a prisoner in the Cause of God, that my life was not wasted, that it was spent in the divine service. Nobody who saw me imagined that I was in prison. They beheld me in the utmost joy, complete thankfulness and health, paying no attention to prison.

# TALK ON THE DAY OF DEPARTURE

*On Board Steamship Celtic,*
*December 5, 1912, New York City.*

This is my last meeting with you, for now I am on the ship ready to sail away. These are my final words of exhortation. I have repeatedly summoned you to the cause of the unity of the world of humanity, announcing that all mankind are the servants of the same God, that God is the Creator of all; He is the Provider and Life-giver; all are equally loved by Him and are His servants upon whom His mercy and compassion descend. Therefore, you must manifest the greatest kindness and love toward the nations of the world, setting aside fanaticism, abandoning religious, national and racial prejudices.

The earth is one native land, one home; and all mankind are the children of one Father. God had created them, and they are the recipients of His compassion. Therefore, if anyone offends another, he offends God. It is the wish of our heavenly Father that every heart should rejoice and be filled with happiness, that we should live together with felicity and joy. The obstacle to human happiness is racial or religious prejudice, the competitive struggle for existence and inhumanity toward each other.

Your eyes have been illumined, your ears are attentive, your hearts knowing. You must be free from prejudice and fanaticism, beholding no differences between the races and religions. You must look to God, for He is the real Shepherd, and all humanity are His sheep. He loves them and loves them equally. As this is true, should the sheep quarrel among themselves? They should manifest gratitude and thankfulness to God, and the best way to thank God is to love one another.

Beware lest ye offend any heart, lest ye speak against anyone in his absence, lest you estrange yourselves from the servants of God. You must consider all His servants as your own family and relations. Direct your whole effort toward the happiness of those who are despondent, bestow food upon the hungry, clothe the needy, and glorify the humble. Be a helper to every helpless one, and manifest kindness to your fellow creatures in order that ye may attain the good pleasure of God. This is conducive to the illumination of the world of humanity and eternal felicity for yourselves. I seek from God everlasting glory in your behalf; therefore, this is my prayer and exhortation.

Consider what is happening in the Balkans. Human blood is being shed, properties are destroyed, possessions pillaged, cities and villages devastated. A world-enkindling fire is astir in the Balkans. God has created men to love each other; but instead they kill each other with cruelty and bloodshed. God has created them that they may cooperate and mingle in accord; but instead, they ravage, plunder and destroy in the carnage of battle. God has created them to be the cause of mutual felicity and peace; but instead, discord, lamentation and anguish arise from the hearts of the innocent and afflicted.

As to you: your efforts must be lofty. Exert yourselves with heart and soul so that, perchance, through your efforts the light of universal peace may shine and this darkness of estrangement and enmity may be dispelled from amongst men, that all men may become as one family and consort together in love and kindness, that the East may assist the West and the West give help to the East, for all are the inhabitants of one planet, the people of one original native land and the flocks of one Shepherd.

Consider how the Prophets who have been sent, the great souls who have appeared and the sages who have arisen in the world have exhorted mankind to unity and love. This has been the essence of their mission and teaching. This has been the goal of their guidance and message. The Prophets, saints, seers and philosophers have sacrificed their lives in order to establish these principles and teachings among men. Consider the heedlessness of the world, for notwithstanding the efforts and sufferings of the Prophets of God, the nations and peoples are still engaged in hostility and fighting. Notwithstanding the heavenly commandments to love one another, they are still shedding each other's blood. How heedless and ignorant are the peoples of the world! How gross the darkness which envelops them! Although they are the children of a compassionate God, they continue to live and act in opposition to His will and good pleasure. God is loving and kind to all men, and yet they show the utmost enmity and hatred toward each other. God is the giver of life to them, and yet constantly seek to destroy life. God blesses and protects their homes; they rage, sack and destroy each other's homes. Consider their ignorance and heedlessness!

Your duty is of another kind, for you are informed of the mysteries of God. Your eyes are illumined; your ears are quickened with hearing. You must, therefore, look toward each other and then toward mankind with the utmost love and kindness. You have no excuse to bring before God if you fail to live according to His command, for you are informed of that which constitutes the good pleasure of God. You have heard His commandments and precepts. You must, therefore, be kind to all men; you must even treat your enemies as your friends. You must consider your evil-wishers as your well-wishers. Those who are not agreeable toward you must be regarded as those who are congenial and pleasant so that, perchance, this darkness of disagreement and conflict may disappear from amongst men and the light of the divine may shine forth, so that the Orient may be illumined and the Occident filled with fragrance, nay, so that East and West may embrace each other in love and deal with one another in sympathy and affection. Until man reaches this high station, the world of humanity shall no find rest, and eternal felicity shall not be attained. But if man lives up to these divine commandments, this world of earth shall be transformed into the world of heaven, and this material sphere shall be converted into a paradise of glory.

It is my hope that you may become successful in this high calling so that like brilliant lamps you may cast light upon the world of humanity and quicken and stir the body of existence like unto a spirit of life. This is eternal glory. This is everlasting felicity. This is immortal life. This is heavenly attainment. This is being created in the image and likeness of God. And into this I call you, praying to God to strengthen and bless you.

# APPENDIX 2

## The Ring, the Pin and the Photographs

In January 1976, Marie and I were working on a Bahá'í exhibit depicting Progressive Revelation to be installed in our neighborhood Public Library and we needed pictures of ancient temples. Chris Filstrup, a Bahá'í friend, was head of the Oriental Dept. of The New York Public Library and was to introduce us to the Ancient Photographs Dept.

The Oriental Dept. has in its collection unique original 19th cent. Bahá'í books, and on appointment day, January 2, Chris said to have just received some Bahá'í books he didn't have time to check yet. While he went with Marie to the photographs room, I looked at the books.

Three of them dated circa 1930 were not significant. But there was a beautiful 1898 leather bound Arabic edition. I opened it, snapshots and letters were inserted between pages. These pictures had informally caught 'Abdu'l-Bahá in various attitudes and walking in Haifa. The letters were dated 1909/1910, one of them seemed to contain something. I opened delicately and there was a rose, still fresh of colors, pink and green and faintly smelling. The letter said: "Dear Asa, I picked up this rose this morning in the garden of 'Abdu'l-Bahá after the Master inhaled its perfume." Hooo! I was ready to put the whole thing in my purse!... Chris said this was "personal property," the Library would keep the book but he had to send the rest to our National Archives in Wilmette. The book was a gift to Asa Cochran, New York 1910.

The name rang a bell. The first Bahá'í book given to me when I first met Bahá'ís in Tacoma, Wash., in 1962, was Not Every Sea Hath Pearls by Loulie Mathews. In the first chapter called "The

*Mrs. Asa Cochran's prayer room described by Mrs. Loulie Mathews in Not Every
Sea Hath Pearls. Mrs. Mathews became a Member of the first official Spiritual
Assembly of the City of New York. Incorporated in 1930, New York Assembly's
bylaws served as legal model for all Bahá'í spiritual Assemblies around the
world. (As described in the hall of Bahá'u'lláh's Mansion of Bahji.)*

Photograph," the author relates being a student of Asa Cochran in 1914, when one day she was told to wait in a small room sparsely furnished with chairs around the photograph of an old gentleman whose stare overpowered her soul.

The following month, our Spiritual Assembly asked us to check weekly on a Bahá'í exhibit celebrating the American Bicentennial installed by the National Spiritual Assembly in the rotunda of Penn Station. On the last Sunday, Michel, Marie's son, then 12 years old, was with us as we planned to visit an antique show on the second floor. Marie went to antique shows searching for old Bahá'í books and Michel was looking for old comics. This was a "bicentennial" show of not much interest to us.

Looking at the last exhibit of jewelry, Michel who was around the display case said: "Hey! There is a Bahá'í ring!" We could not see it and had to bend toward Michel's height to see a tiny gold ring with a brown stone: sure it was!... I asked for the price, crossing my fingers that I could afford it... The lady dealer said that this was a 200 years old ring. "It cannot be, this is a Bahá'í ring and the Faith started in 1844." "Are you Bahá'í? The stone may be Bahá'í, but the setting is older with that carving - one owl on each side, wings spread out toward the stone. The owl is an Indian symbol of wisdom in Washington State and this ring belonged to the Cochran family." We were stunned!

Mrs. Reiner, explained the mystery. The Cochrans were part of the American lore in Washington State where they made their fortune. They moved to New York in 1896 and Mrs. Cochran traveled around the world with their two young daughters who gave concerts as "musical prodigies". They lost their fortune during the Depression. The younger daughter, Olea, had died penniless this past December. The City of New York auctioned her house and estate. Books went to the Main Public Library, where we found their Bahá'í books, and antique dealers bought the rest by lots.

Mrs. Reiner had bought boxes of letters bearing the name "Abd... Abd...," "'Abdu'l-Bahá?" "Yes." As a Jewish person, she had been interested to read some of these letters from the Holy Land

and she had kept one box with photographs that she would be glad to give to us as Bahá'ís, we would only pay a nominal price for the frames. She sold me the ring "at a discount" and gave us her New Jersey address.

This was a very moving encounter. The photographs in that box were taken during 'Abdu'l-Bahá's visit to New York in 1912. One of them, an original had the Master's signature and another was the work of renowned Gertrude Käsebier with a full sentence in Persian written by 'Abdu'l-Bahá. There was also a radiant gold pin which Marie could buy. It was engraved with the Greatest Name and a Persian writing on the back. The box contained some letters, translations of 'Abdu'l-Bahá's tablets. Three of them, dated 1909, were addressed to Mrs. Cochran asking her to travel to India for the Faith.

Our Bahá'í friends were all excited by this amazing treasure-trove. We learned the translation of the Master's handwriting on the photograph:

"O Lord, this handmaiden is working in Thy service, make her victorious."

This was probably addressed to Mrs. Cochran who had traveled for the Faith. The engraving on the back of the pin: "Khátam Awliya" means "Symbol of the Saints," and may be associated with the name "Olea".

When living in Los Angeles, in 1965, at a time of trial, after praying 'Abdu'l-Bahá for guidance, I had a dream in which a veiled Being, surrounded by light, was giving me this tiny brown ring. But, now we were not sure we should keep these precious objects.

We showed the whole treasure to Hand of the Cause Mr. Khádem, who was very moved. He raised the ring, the pin and the photographs to his brow, praying. He confirmed that the small brown stone was one of the cornelians 'Abdu'l-Bahá had engraved to His specifications to give to friends for their services to the Faith. The inscriptions on the pin were also from the Master. We were deeply grateful for these gifts from beyond the grave, but what shall we do now? Mr. Khádem assured us: "You found them, 'Abdu'l-

Bahá wanted you to have them for some reason, they are yours to keep."

We thought that it was tragic we never learned of the plight of this family. Yet, our "finding" of these precious heirlooms may mean that these friends found peace and reward in the Abhá Kingdom.

The photograph commented upon in Mrs. Mathews' book was of Juliet Thompson's portrait of 'Abdu'l-Bahá. We have it now, in its ebony frame, as shown in the picture of a makeshift altar as described in the book.

Since 1972, when I first read the typescript of Juliet Thompson's diaries, I was making researches and gathering material on 'Abdu'l-Bahá's 1912 visit to New York for teaching purpose. The finding of this treasure, confirmed my resolve to write a book. These 1912 photographs are now in this book, perhaps the reason we found them was for us to give them back to the community of the City of the Covenant.

Eliane Lacroix-Hopson, with
her daughter, Marie-Danielle Samuel,
and her grandson, Michel G. Samuel.

# PLACES 'ABDU'L-BAHA VISITED

**During His 1912 trip to New York, the City of the Covenant, in order of visit or appearance.**
*(Some of these buildings do not exist anymore.)*

Ansonia Hotel, Broadway and 73rd Street : 9-day stay.

780 West End Avenue. Home of Mr. and Mrs. Edward B. Kinney: The Master's headquarters for Bahá'í activities; His residence May 26-30.

935 Eastern Parkway, Brooklyn. Home of Mr. and Mrs. Howard MacNutt.

36 West 67th Street. Studio of Miss Phillips.

141 East 2lst Street. Home of Mr. and Mrs. Alexander Morten.

Church of the Ascension, 5th Avenue and 10th Street. First official appearance and subsequent People Forum.

Camegie Lyceum, (now Carnegie Hall) Union Meeting of Advanced Thought Center, West 57th Street.

327 West End Avenue. Home of Mr. and Mrs. Mountfort Mills.

261 West 139th Street. Home of Mr. and Mrs. Arthur Dodge.

1943 East 16th Street, Brooklyn. Home of Mr. and Mrs. William Dodge.

273 West 90th Street. Home of Mr. and Mrs. Marshall L. Emery, was also the Master's residence December 1-5.

Little Theatre, West 44th Street. Performance "The Terrible Meek," the Master was invited by playwright Charles Rand Kennedy.

Earl Hall, Columbia University. 'Abdu'l-Bah· on Religion and Science.

227 Bowery, Bowery Mission. The Master spoke to 400 derelicts and distributed money.

227 Riverside Drive, Hudson Apartment House, His residence May 11-26.

Unity Church, Montclair, N.J.

Grace Methodist Episcopal Church, West 104th Street. International Peace Forum.

Hotel Astor, Reception New York Peace Society.

Lake Mohonk, N. Y. National Conference of Peace and International Arbitration.

Church of the Divine Paternity, Central Park West.

Brotherhood Church, Jersey City, N.J.

Metropolitan Temple, 7th Avenue and 14th Street. Woman's Suffrage and major Peace events.

130 West 57th Street. Home of Mr. and Mrs. Tatum.

Mount Morris Baptist Church (now Mount Moriah), 5th Avenue and 126th Street.

309 West 78th Street. House of Mr. and Mrs. Frank Champney, rented main residence of 'Abdu'l-Bahá, June 1st to July 23; November 11-30.

Theosophical Society, Broadway and 79th Street.

New York University.

Town Hall, Fanwood, NJ.

Union League Club, Bedford Square, Brooklyn.

316 Bedford Avenue, Brooklyn. Home of Mr. and Mrs. Frank Newton.

Fourth Unitarian Church, Beverly Road, Brooklyn.

Central Congregational Church. Hancock Street, Brooklyn.

West Englewood, N.J. Home of Mr. and Mrs. J. 0. Wilhelm and Roy Wilhelm, Site of the Unity Feat.

Morristown, N.J. Home of Hon. H. H. Topakyan, Consul General of Persia.

Walnut Crescent, Montclair, N.J. Home of Mr. and Mrs. Charles Edsall.

American Museum of Natural History. New York City.

95th Street and West End Avenue. Home of Mr. and Mrs. Harris.

48 West 10th Street. Home of Juliet Thompson.

All Souls Unitarian Church. Fourth Avenue and 20th Street.
830 Park Avenue. Home of Dr. and Mrs. Florian Krug.
Genealogical Hall, 226 West 58th Street.
J. Pierpont Morgan Library, Madison Avenue and 36th Street.
575 Riverside Drive. Home of Mr. and Mrs. Frank K. Moxey.
Great Northern Hotel, 118 West 57th Street. Day of the Covenant
    Banquet, on November 23.
Waldorf Astoria Hotel, Club Minerva Reception.
542 West 114th Street. Home of Mrs. Asa Cochran.

# SELECTED BIBLIOGRAPHY

'Abdu'l-Bahá. Promulgation of Universal Peace. Wilmette, IL: Bahá'í Publishing Trust, 1982.

Bahá'í Publishing Trust. 'Abdu'l-Bahá Glimpses of Perfection. Film strip, 1971.

Bahá'í Publishing Trust. The Bahá'í World, An International Record. Vol. IX, 1945, Vol. XII, 1956, Vol. IV, 1933 Wilmette, IL, Reprinted 1981.

Balyuzi, H.M. 'Abdu'l-Bahá. London : George Ronald, 1971.

Gail, Marzieh. Juliet Remembers Gibran. Wilmette, IL: World Order Magazine, 1978.

Gibran, Jean and Kahlil. Kahlil Gibran His Life and World. New York: Avenell Books, 1981.

Ives, Howard Colby. Portals To Freedom. London: George Ronald, 1962.

Mathews, Loulie Albee. Not Every Sea Hath Pearls. Colorado Spring, 1951.

McComb, Robert. 'Abdu'l-Bahá In New York. New York State Bulletin, 1977.

Morisson, Gayle. To Move The World, Louis Gregory and the Advancement of Racial Unity in America. Wilmette, IL: Bahá'í Publishing Trust, 1982.

Shoghi Effendi. God Passes By. Wilmette, IL: Bahá'í Publishing Trust, 1957.

Star of the West. Vol. II, III, IV, Bahá'í Magazine, 1911-1913. Reprinted, Oxford: George Ronald, 1976.

The Spiritual Assembly of the Bahá'ís of the City of New York. 'Abdu'l-Bahá In New York. New York, 1932.

The Universal House of Justice. The Bahá'í World, An International Record. Vol. XIII, Haifa: 1970.

Thompson, Juliet. The Diary of Juliet Thompson. Los Angeles : Kalimat Press, 1983.

Ward, Allan L. 239 Days: 'Abdu'l-Bahá's Journey in America. Wilmette, IL.: Bahá'í Publishing Trust, 1979.

Young, Barbara. This Man From Lebanon. New York: A.A. Knopf, 1945.

Zarqani, Mahmud. Diary of Abdu'l-Bahá's Travels in Europe and America. Vol.1. Known in the West as "Mahmud's Diary". Typescript Copy: The Archives of the Spiritual Assembly of the Bahá'ís of the City of New York. (Originally published, Bombay, 1914.)

# NOTES

ABBREVIATIONS:

M p.#        Mahmud's Diary; typescript copy.
JT p.#       Diary of Juliet Thompson; Kalimat Press Edition.
PF p.#       Portals To Freedom, 1962 Edition.
S/W date     Star of the West.
PUP p#       Promulgation of Universal Peace, Compilation of 'Abdu'l-
             Bahá's addresses.
AW p.#       Allan L. Ward's "239 Days."

**(Endnotes)**

1   S/W Bahá'í News, Oct. 16, 1910.
2   M12-3; 'Abdu'l-Bahá (Balyuzi) p. 172.
3   Not Every Sea Hath Pearls, p.142.
4   S/W lll, April 28, 1912, p. 3-5
5   JT233-6; PUP 33.
6   M21-2; JT239; PUP4-9; PF33.
7   M24-6; JT244-8; PUP14-6; S/W lll, April 28, 1912, p.5-6.
8   World Order, Summer 1978. p. 29-31; This Man from Lebanon p.
    68-9.
9   M24-7; S/W III, Sept.8, 1912. p.7-9; PUP18-29
10  M27; JT262-7; AW27-36.
11  M33-4, 55; JT284; PUP111-12.
12  M57-63; JT285; S/W lll, Aug. 1, 1912. p. 10-5; PUPII 3-26.
13  M63-4; S/W ll, Dec.12.1911, p.3-5; 'Abdu'l-Bahá In New York, NY
    State Bulletin, Part 5&6.
14  M65-6; JT287-8; S/W III, Aug. 20,1912, p.6; PUP129-137.
15  JT288-93.

16  M66-71; JT296.

17  M72-3; S/W lll, July 13, 1912, p. 14-21; PUP150-60; God Passes By p. 289.

18  M74-5; JT297-8; PUP163-71

19  M75-7; JT 300.

10  M74; JT298-9; PUP161-3.

21  M78-82; JT 302-4; 308-10; PUP189-90; S/W lll, Sept. 8, 1912, p.17.

22  M83-4; PUP190-205.

23  M85; S/W lll, Sept.8, 1912, 3-4. Mr. Roy Wilhelm was associated with the technical realization of the film and recording with Special Event Film Company and Columbia Gramophone Company, both firms in New York City

24  'Abdu'l-Bahá (Balyuzi) p. 220. On April 26- 30, 1919, the Annual Bah·'í Convention was held at the McAlpin Hotel in New York. 'Abdu'l-Bahá had previously cabled and asked that this convention be called "The Convention of the Covenant," because it was to be the occasion of the unveiling of the "Tablets of the Divine Plan." These tablets, revealed between 1916-17, were kept in the vaults of the Shrine of the Bab on Mount Carmel during the war years. 'Abdu'l-Bah· (Balyuzi), p. 434.

25  JT311-6

26  S/W lll, Nov. 23, 1912 p. 15.

27  M85; 'Abdu'l-Bahá (Balyuzi) pp. 149, 151, 220

28  M92; JT 322-4.

29  M94; AW105-7.

30  M95-8; JT325-6, 353-4

31  JT328-336; PF63-7.

32  M102-4; JT345.

33  M105; PF94; JT 350-2

34  M106-8; AW 116.

35  M74: SIWIII, Oct.16. 1912, p.15. 'Abdu'l-Bahá made the announcement at an interracial gathering. " The white persons were astonished to see the influence of the Cause and the colored were very pleased... This was little less than a miracle; in fact the splitting of the moon in two pieces seemed an easier accomplishment to the eyes of the Americans."

36 To Move The World: Louis Gregory and The Advancement of Racial Unity in +America, pp.63-8. This is a biography of the great man who, supported by his wife, sacrificed all to their common goal of serving the Faith in the crucial area of racial unity, "the most challenging issue in this country," in the words of Shoghi Effendi. Mr. Gregory is known in the Bahá'i World as a "Hand of the Cause of God," the highest title accorded to an individual believer in the Faith.

37 JT 364-7. The husband of Mrs. Krug, Dr. Florian Krug, a renowned physician, was very hostile to the Faith. He changed completely after meeting 'Abdu'l-Bahá and became a devoted believer. He was on pilgrimage with his wife in November 1921, and had the privilege of closing the eyes of the Master on His deathbed, November 28, 1921. 'Abdu'l-Bahá, (Balyuzi) 452.

38 M151; JT 368.

39 M152-3; AW186-7.

40 M155; JT375-6; PUP447-8

41 M156; JT376-80.

42 JT 384

43 M158-61; PUP452-3

44 M162-4; JT389-91; PUP462-70.

45 M165; JT393.

46 God Passes By, p. 280.

# BAHAI HEAD ARRIVES

Abdul Baha Abbas Guest in National Capital.

## RECEPTION IS TENDERED

To Speak Before Persian-American Educational Society.

## OUTLINES HIS AMBITIONS

Object of Life to Promote Oneness of Life and World-Wide Peace.

Abdul Baha Abbas, world leader of the Bahai movement, who has been in the United States for a fortnight, at the beginning of a tour of the *principal cities* of the country, reached West *afternoon from New York*. For *a part of the afternoon he will be present at Reacher's* at a reception and musical to be given in his honor, and in consequence of the general invitation which has been extended to the public to attend this function, it is expected many Bahais and their friends will take advantage of the opportunity to greet the distinguished Persian. Abdul Baha tonight will be one of the speakers at the closing session in the Public Library lecture hall of the second annual conference of the Persian-American Educational Society.

In an interview soon after he reached the city Abdul Baha declared that his primary object in coming to America was to see the country.

### Discloses Ambitions.

"Last year I went to London and Paris and saw three cities, and then returned to Egypt," he said. "Now I have come to America to see this country, for I have heard many wonderful praises and commendations of America, that it is a country well populated and well civilized. People here enjoy freedom and liberty.

"On the other hand I have heard that in America many great *societies* organizations are being formed for international peace and arbitration. It is my highest desire to see these societies and concur with their founders and members. The great object of my life is to promote the oneness of the kingdom of humanity and international peace."

Replying to a question whether a person with a religion—Christian, Mohammedan or Jewish—could follow the Bahai teachings without abandoning his religion, Abdul Baha said:

"Yes, for truth is always one. The

# Unitarians Rise to Greet Persian Speaker at Tremont Temple

THE BOSTON TRAVELER, FRIDAY, MAY 24, 1912

# Abdul Baha Has Creed He Declares Will Finally Eliminate Criminal

## PERSIAN EXPLAINS PLAN TO UNITE ALL RELIGIONS

Abdul Baha Abbas, Exiled Philosopher, Says America Is Behind in Spiritual Civilization.

By the Associated Press.

NEW YORK, April 14.—Abdul Abbas, the venerable Persian philosopher and religious leader, who is head of the Bahai movement for the unification of religions, and for the establishment of universal peace, made his first public address in America to-day at the Church of the Ascension in Fifth avenue. He spoke through an interpreter, his nephew Dr. Ameen Ullah Fareed, on "The Baha Revelation."

Abdul Baha Abbas recently arrived here from Egypt. Rev. Dr. Percy Stickney Grant, rector of the church, in introducing Abdul Baha, who is an exile from his country, welcomed him as a "messenger from the east, freshly bearing *a message* of the gospel of peace, good will and love to all mankind."

### URGES RELIGIOUS UNITY.

Abdul Baha Abbas, Leader of the Bahai Movement, Arrives in New York to Propagate the Cult.

[BY A. P. NIGHT WIRE TO THE TIMES]

NEW YORK, April 11.—Abdul Baha Abbas, the leader of the Bahai movement for world-wide religious unity, arrived here early to-day on the steamer Cedric from the Mediterranean. Preparations for his welcome at the pier were made yesterday by the Persian-American Educational Society and a number of local followers.

# PERSIAN PEACE APOSTLE PREDICTS WAR IN EUROPE

Abdul Baha Urges Local Bahaists to Do All in Their Power to Avert Terrible Bloodshed Which He Says Is Pending in East.

Warning against a great European war and pleading that the people of this country do what they can to avert terrible bloodshed, Abdul Baha,

## Persian Does Not Believe in Capital Punishment and Thinks That, in Education, Woman Should Have Preference Over Mere Man.

"No, I do not believe in capital punishment," said Abdul Baha, founder of the new Bahai religious movement, to-day in an interview with the Traveler.

"If the Bahai movement is widely

this government is fair."
"International peace today greatest issue of

# ABDUL BAHA ARRIVES IN UNITED STATES

HEAD OF THE BAHAI'ST SECT WHICH HAS 14,000,000 ADHERENTS HERE

## IN JAIL FIFTY YEARS

*Because* of His Religious Views the Greater Portion of His Life Has Been Spent Behind Prison Walls

(Star Special)
Chicago, April 26.—Abdul Baha, head of the Bahaist sect, which, although originating in Persia, now has over 14,000,000 adherents in all parts of the world, has come all the way from Russia to address the faithful American Congress of Baha-

# PERSIAN INTERESTED IN AFRICAN CAUSE

National Association for the Advancement of Colored People Will Begin Fourth Annual Convention Tonight.

## MISS JANE ADDAMS WILL PRESIDE AT FIRST SESSION

Noted Speakers Will Appear Before Conference and Discuss Mob Law and Lynchings—Initial Meeting in the West.

# AGED PERSIAN, A PRISONER FOR HALF A CENTURY, COMES TO AMERICA TO PREACH THE GOSPEL OF UNIVERSAL RELIGION

## ASSAILS BAHAI LEADER AND PERSIAN VERACITY

### Dr. C. Ernest Smith Declares Missionary Should Not Be Encouraged.

MAN WHO ADVOCATES WHAT IS GOOD IN ALL RELIGIONS. TALKS ON MODERN CONDITIONS AND TELLS WHY POLITICS CAN NOT ADVANCE UNTIL WOMEN HAVE RIGHT TO VOTE

Out of prison comes the first missionary from the east to the west. His name is Abdul Baha Abbas, and he spent 56 of his 67 years in prison. He comes to preach the oneness of God, the oneness of religion, the oneness of mankind, the eradication of war and the establishment of universal peace ...

## TELLS OF BAHAI IDEALS

### Abdul Baha Portrays Principles of Order of Which He Is Head.

The portrayal of the principles of the Bahai movement was the feature of a public meeting which was held at D. A. R. Continental Memorial Hall last night. Abdul Baha, world-leader of the Bahais, was the principal speaker, and the meeting, which was held under the auspices of the Orient-Occident Unity, marked his last public appearance in the National Capital on his present tour of the eastern states.

*Washington, N. Y. Press.*
*Monday, April 15, 1912*

## ABDUL BAHA TO PREACH —PEACE TO AMERICANS

### Persian Philosopher, Leader of Bahai Movement, to Urge One Religion for All Men

New York, April 14.—The accomplishment of a task which many leaders have undertaken, but at which none has succeeded, the bringing about of universal peace and a single religion among all men, is the professed purpose of Abdul Baha, famous Persian philosopher and leader of the Bahai movement, who came to this country from Alexandria, Egypt, yesterday on board the steamer of the White Star Line.

Abdul Baha will begin his work of converting America at the Peace Conference at Lake Mohonk late this month, and thereafter will be heard at colleges, churches and gatherings of earnest persons throughout the land.

Abdul Baha's philosophy is of a sort which the Occidental mind does not grasp in the first sentence. Universal peace and oneness of religion, he said yesterday, exist rather in the inner man than in his circumstances of time, place, race or condition of servitude, and he who loves his fellow man with all his heart and has shaken off the fetters of "self-imprisonment" is both free and a communicant in the universal religion.

"For instance," he said, with a gesture in the direction of the Statue of Liberty, "there is your country's emblem of peace and justice toward all. But I know that peace and justice are not a matter of race and country. Happiness is not holiness only who loves his native land, but who loves all humanity."

It was explained for Abdul Baha through his nephew, Dr. Ameen Fareed who interprets him, that no man in the world has had more cause to despair of peace and justice than his uncle. Until last Summer, when he visited Paris and London, he had been immured for 40 years, a prisoner in a fortress at Acre, Syria. The Young Turks party, after the overthrow of Abdul Hamid, brought about his release. He was sent to Acre with his father, Baha Ullah, founder of the Bahai movement, when he was a young man.

One proof of his uncle's devotion to the ideal of universal justice, Dr. ...

ABDUL BAHA.

## BAHAIST LEADER HERE TO HELP WORLD PEACE

### Abdul Baha to Talk With Men Who Are Working for Wiping Out of War.

### HIS DOCTRINE ONE OF LOVE

### When Women Are Highly Cultivated There Will Be No Difference in Sexes.

*N. Y. Courier.*
*Monday, April 15, 1912*

### WESTERN WORLD BEHIND IN SPIRITUAL CIVILIZATION

### Persian Philosopher and Religious Leader, Head of Bahaists, Addresses New York Audience

New York, April 14.—Abdul Baha, the venerable Persian philosopher and religious leader, who is head of the Bahai movement for the unification of religions and for the establishment of universal peace, made his first public address in America today at the Church of the Ascension on Fifth avenue. He spoke through an interpreter, his nephew.

The Rev. Dr. Francis E. Clark, founder of the Christian Endeavor Society, and Dr. John E. Robinson, bishop of Bombay, were passengers on the same steamer with Abbas Effendi.

## ABDUL BAHA ABBAS MAKES FIRST SPEECH

### Persian Philosopher Says Spiritual Civilization Alone Can Produce Peace

The fourth annual conference of the National Association for the Advancement of Colored People will begin tonight at the new Sinai temple Forty-fifth street, and ...

The program for the first session, which Miss Jane Addams will preside, will consist of addresses by Oswald Garrison Villard of New York, William Pickens of Talladega, Ala., and Abdul Baha, whose presence will testify to the sympathy of the Persians in the cause of the African ...

*Philadelphia, Pa., Inquirer.*
*Monday, April 15, 1912*

## BAHAS COMING TO DISCUSS WAR

### Universal Religion Delegates Begin Sessions in Boston

Abbas Effendi, as he is known by his official title, is the third of the leaders of Bahaism. He has been repeatedly imprisoned by the Moslems, who regard his liberal tendencies with the greatest distrust. The Bahai belief is that universal peace is possible only through the harmony of all religions, and that all religions are basically one. It is estimated that about a third of the Persians are now members of the cult.

The Rev. Dr. Francis E. Clark, founder of the Christian Endeavor Society, and Dr. John E. Robinson, bishop of Bombay, were passengers on the same steamer with Abbas Effendi.

## ABDUL BAHA READY TO FACE MALCONTENTS

### Will Stand Heckling Here June 18; Departs for Cleveland to Preach Peace.

Abdul Baha, master of the Bahaist movement and exponent of universal peace and the brotherhood of man, showed no anxiety yesterday when asked concerning the test questions he is expected to answer at the forthcoming peace conference of the Bahai ...

*Baltimore, Md., Sun.*
*Monday, April 15, 1912*

## ABDUL BAHA WITHIN WEEK

### Persian Philosopher Will Speak in This City.

Abdul Baha Abbas, the Persian philosopher, expected to arrive in Baltimore within the next week and the Baltimore followers of the Bahai movement are making ...

*Washington, D. C., Herald*

## FLAYS BAHA'S PREACHING.

"Prophetic Evangelist" Avails ...

*Los Angeles, Cal., Times.*
*Friday, April 12, 1912*

## URGES RELIGIOUS UNITY.

### Abdul Baha Abbas, Leader of the Bahai Movement, Arrives in New York to Propagate the Cult.

(BY A P. NIGHT WIRE TO THE TIMES.)

NEW YORK.—Abdul Baha Abbas, the leader of the Bahai movement for world-wide religious unity, arrived here early today on the steamer Cedric from the Mediterranean. Preparations for his welcome at the pier were made yesterday by the Persian-American Educational Societies and a number of local followers.

Abbas Effendi, as he is known by his official title, is the third of the leaders of Bahaism. He has been repeatedly imprisoned by the Moslems who regard his liberal tendencies with the greatest distrust. The Bahai belief is that universal peace is possible only through the harmony of all religions, and that all religions are basically one. It is estimated that about a third of the Persians are now members of the cult.

The Rev. Dr. Francis E. Clark, founder of the Christian Endeavor Society, and Dr. John E. Robinson, bishop of Bombay, were passengers on the same steamer with Abbas Effendi.

## PERSIAN TEACHER, ABDUL BAHA ABBAS SCENTS GREAT ...

### So Called Prophet of Peace Buffalonians to ...

# Persian, Hailed as New "Messiah," Comes to Teach Unity of the World

Baltimore, Md., Eve Sun
Friday, April 12, 1912

## Abdul Baha, Invited to Visit Cleveland by Followers Here—Head of Sect Which Boasts That 50,000 Members Have Died for Their Faith in Less Than Seventy Years—Leader Prisoner Since Youth.

"What hath God wrought!"
These words of Samuel F. Morse sent tingling over the world's first telegraph line between Washington and Baltimore, heralded the birth of Abdul Baha Abbas.

Such is the belief of the 2,400,000 followers of the Persian philosopher and teacher of a new religious cult, who is now on a visit to the United States, and who is expected to include Cleveland in his itinerary.

Abdul Baha, son of Baha Ullah, whose coming was foretold by Bab, a religious revolutionist, who followers claim was a John the Baptist, for their belief was born on the same day that the first telegraph message was sent. Bahaists place a new meaning upon the words of Morse, the inventor.

Although the new cult is less than sixty years old, 50,000 of its members have died as martyrs to their faith in Persia and Turkey. Abdul Baha has a considerable following in Cleveland. Meetings are held each Wednesday evening at the home of Dr. Charles M. Swingle, 2805 Wade Park

## ABDUL BAHA COMING TO CHICAGO MEETING

### Leader of Bahai Movement, Which Is Attracting Nations of the World, Is Guest in America.

### CHARITY AND PEACE SOUGHT

### Universal Brotherhood of Man and the Unity of Religious Creeds Also Objects of Search.

Abdul Baha, which is not a name, but a title, signifying "servant of God," the remarkable Persian who is at the head of the Bahai movement, which has spread to all corners of the world, and who arrived in New York yesterday on his first visit to this country, will come to Chicago on April 27 to attend the international congress of the Bahai movement and Chicago adherents of the movement are making preparations for his reception. Delegates are expected from Honolulu and other parts of the globe, as well as from assemblies in various parts of the United States.

The congress will open on the evening of the arrival of Abdul Baha with a reception to the leader and visiting delegates and will continue, according to present plans for five days. On the final day the woman's Bahai assembly will give a reception to the club women of Chicago in the red ballroom of the Hotel La Salle, and Abdul Baha will address the women. In this connection it may be stated that he is in favor of woman suffrage, being an advocate of equality for women, not in politics only, but in all things else.

### Teaches Brotherhood of Man.

The movement, although it orig...

Noted Persian, Bahaian Move Leader

Abdul Baha, who will address followers in Chicago on peace and universal brotherhood

GREAT PERSIAN HERE

### Leader Of Bahai Movement Makes First Visit To The Western World

[From the New York Times]

Abdul Baha, a distinguished Persian, at the head of the Bahai movement for the unification of religions, arrived in New York on the White Star liner Cedric yesterday. It is his first visit to the United States, and, with the single exception of a short visit to Paris and London last summer, this is the first time in more than 40 years he has left the "prison city" of Acre, in Syria, to which he and his father, Ben Ullah, the founder of the Bahai movement, were exiled by the Turkish Government 50 years ago.

Abdul Baha comes to us on a mission of peace and will deliver one of his principal addresses before the Peace Conference at Lake Mohonk the latter part of this month, after which he will deliver addresses before various peace societies, religious organizations and educational bodies. As he puts it, he is ready to speak "wherever an audience can be found to welcome peace and promote the realization of the brotherhood of man."

When the reporters boarded the Cedric off Quarantine yesterday morning they found Abdul Baha on the upper deck. He was dressed in a long, flowing black Oriental gown, underneath which was another of a light tan color. On his head he wore a snow-white turban. He gave the reporters a hearty welcome, and he proved such a good talker that there was no occasion to ask questions. He talked of newspapers, of woman suffrage, of universal peace, of religion and of Persia. He began with newspapers.

"The pages of swiftly appearing newspapers," said Abdul Baha, "are indeed the mirror of the world. They display the doings and actions of the different nations; they both illustrate them and cause them to be heard. Newspapers are as a mirror which is endowed with hearing, sight and speech; they are wonderful phenomena. But it behooveth editors to be sanctified from the prejudice of egotism and desire, and to be adorned with the ornaments of unity and justice. There are good newspapers and likewise bad ones. Those that strive to tell only the truth are like the sun, for they light the world everywhere and their work is imperishable. Those that play for their own little selfish ends give no true light to the world and perish of their own futility."

When the Cedric was opposite the Statue of Liberty Abdul Baha extended his arms in a salute and referred to his ever long exile in Syria. He talked of world-wide peace, which he termed the greatest of all causes. The diversity of faiths and the lack of universal auxiliary languages he mentioned as the obstacles that are to be surmounted in the attainment of the peace program.

...interrupted to ask

### Free Coin on Bowery.

An incident that might have been immortalized by a literary were he still alive, occurred on the East Side last night, when Abdul Baha, the Persian prophet, attired in the flowing robes of the Far East, visited the Bowery Mission. "Bagdad on the Subway" as O. Henry often called New York, has been the scene of countless incidents that might be woven into tales as fascinating as those related to Haroun-al-Raschid, and many of them have been enacted in the Bowery.

At the end of his address Abdul Baha said he would like to meet each man as he passed out of the building. He said he had a token for them. Again the eyes of all followed him as he passed down the stair and took a station near the door, carrying a mysterious looking bag in his hand.

As each man passed the prophet he was allowed to grasp his hand and as he withdrew it to his palm lay a bright silver quarter.

Four hundred men were in the hall, and there was a gift for all. After the last man had gone and the empty bag remained, Abdul Baha congratulated the leaders of the mission and expressed his pleasure at having been able to be there.

Outside, on the Bowery, the news that there was a "guy givin' away quarters at the mission" spread like wildfire, a crowd that included outside of the town battled ... projects the door, but $100 in current dimes was all the change the good prophet happened to have about him.

# PERSIAN INTERESTED IN AFRICAN CAUSE

National Association for the Advancement of Colored People Will Begin Fourth Annual Convention Tonight.

## MISS JANE ADDAMS WILL PRESIDE AT FIRST SESSION

Noted Speakers Will Appear Before Conference and Discuss Mob Law and Lynchings—Initial Meeting in the West.

The fourth annual conference of the National Association for the Advancement of Colored People will begin tonight in the new Shiloh temple Forty-sixth street, and Second boulevard.

The program for the first session, which Miss Jane Addams will preside, will consist of addresses by Oswald Garrison Villard of New York, W. L. de Pleasant of Talladega, Ala., and others. Dr. W. E. B. DuBois, editor of the Crisis, the organ of the association.

# BAHAIS COMING TO DISCUSS WAR

Universal Religion Delegates Begin Sessions In Boston

# ABDUL BAHA ARRIVES IN UNITED STATES

HEAD OF THE BAHAIST SECT, WHICH HAS 11,000,000 ADHERENTS HERE.

## IN JAIL FIFTY YEARS

because of His Religious Views the Greater Portion of His Life Has Been Spent Behind Prison Walls

(Star Special)

Chicago, April 26.—Abdul Baha, head of the Bahaist sect which although originating in Persia has had over 11,000,000 adherents in all parts of the world, has called all the faithful of the American Congress of Bahaists, which will open here tomorrow or a session of a week. The aged Persian spent half a century of his life in prison, on account of his religious views and his attempts to convert the Mohammedans to the new faith, which, it is declared, embraces all that is best in all religions. Abdul Baha, whose father was the prophet and principal founder of the cult, says his purpose is to unite all religions in one. Before returning to Persia, he will address the Lake Mohonk, N. Y., Peace Conference the middle of next month. He is an advocate of universal peace, believes in woman's rights, and is otherwise socially and politically progressive. While in Chicago Abdul Baha will indicate the new Mashrak-El-Azkar, the first "temple of unity" to be built

Cleveland, Ohio, Plain dealer
Monday, April 15, 1912

# HEAD OF BIG CULT WAS OFTEN JAILED

Abdul Baha Abbas, Who is to Visit Cleveland on Tour, Was Often Victim of Abdul Hamid's Ire.

Cleveland soon will receive as its guest the founder of a new religious cult, who, like the founder of almost all religious cults, comes from the Orient. Abdul Baha Abbas, who claims to have a following of about 11,000,000 people in all parts of the world, has arrived in New York city on his tour of the world.

Abdul Baha, the son of Baha'o'llah, whose coming was foretold by Bab, a religious revolutionist who lived almost a century ago and gained the frowns of the Persian government because of his doctrine, has spent much of his life in imprisonment. His incarceration was due largely to the dislike of Abdul Hamid, the deposed ruler of Turkey.

Abdul Hamid maintained that the preachings of Abdul Baha were contrary to the teachings of the Mohammedan religion. For forty-two years he kept the prophet under surveillance, most of that time in solitary confinement. The Persian ruler of whom Abdul Baha is a subject, would not interfere because he is a follower of the same faith as Abdul Hamid.

Despite his sixty-eight years and many hardships endured, the Persian still is spry and takes an active interest in everything that he sees. After being taken from the boat to the hotel in New York city he toured the city in a taxicab. The great crowds of busy people and the many women on the streets impressed him so he dubbed New York the "beehive" city.

ABDUL BAHA ABBAS

# PERSIAN PEACE APOSTLE PREDICTS WAR IN EUROPE

Abdul Baha Urges Local Bahaists to Do All in Their Power to Avert Terrible Bloodshed Which He Says Is Pending in East.

Warning against a great European war and pleading that this country do what they can to avert terrible bloodshed, Abdul Baha, head of the Bahaist movement, addressed the Bahaists, which will open here tomorrow or a session of a week. The aged Persian spent half a century of his life in prison, on account of his religious views and his attempts to convert the Mohammedans to the new faith, which, it is declared, embraces all that is best in all religions. Abdul Baha, whose father was the prophet and principal founder of the cult, says his purpose is to unite all religions in one. Before returning to Persia, he will address the Lake Mohonk, N. Y., Peace Conference the middle of next month. He is an advocate of universal peace, believes in woman's rights, and is otherwise socially and politically progressive. While in Chicago Abdul Baha will indicate the new Mashrak-El-Azkar, the first "temple of unity" to be built of the Bahaists in America. In addition to the nine-sided structure for religious worship, there will be four other buildings on the grounds, one hospice for entertaining traveling Bahaists, another a hospital, a third school for orphans, and the fourth home for the aged. In the Bahai movement there are no paid teachers, as all teach and all work. Abdul Baha advocates that all Bahais, whatever Catholic, Protestant, etc.

## "ALL MEN ARE ONE."

PHILADELPHIA, Pa.—(A. P.).—"The greatest, the most recent discovery of the aged is that all men are as said Albert Vail of Chicago, an address last night in Witherspoon Hall, at the convention for Negroes. White and Colored Races.

# BAHA PLEADS FOR NATIONS LEAGUE

October 6, 1919

Leader of Cult Founded on Brotherhood of Man Writes From Syria to Ex-Gov. Sulzer.

Abdul Baha Abbas, the leader of the religious movement based on the bretherhood of man, which started in Persia two generations ago and has spread surprisingly in different part of the world, has written to former Gov. Sulzer a letter strongly favoring the League of Nations. The letter is in response to an inquiry by Mr. Sulzer.

# ABDUL BAHA TO PREACH —PEACE TO AMERICANS

Persian Philosopher, Leader of Babel Movement, to Urge One Religion for All Men

New York, April 12.—The accomplishment of a task which many headliners have undertaken, but at which none has succeeded, the bringing about of universal peace and a single religion among all men, is the professed purpose of Abdul Baha, famous Persian philosopher and leader of the Babel movement, who came to this country from Alexandria, Egypt, yesterday on board the Cedric, of the White Star Line.

Abdul Baha will begin his work of converting America at the Peace conference at Lake Mohonk late this month, and thereafter will be at colleges, churches and gatherings of persons throughout the

# BAHAIST LEADER HERE TO HELP WORLD PEACE

Abdul Baha to Talk With Men Who Are Working for Wiping Out of War.

## HIS DOCTRINE ONE OF LOVE

When Women Are Highly Cultivated There Will Be No Difference in Sexes.

2ND ED'N. N. Y. Courier.
Monday, April 15, 1912

### WESTERN WORLD BEHIND IN SPIRITUAL CIVILIZATION

Persian Philosopher and Religious Leader, Head of Bahaism, Addresses New York Audience.

New York, April 16.—Abdul Baha Abbas, the venerable Persian philosopher and religious leader, who is head of the Bahai movement for the unification of religions and for the establishment of universal peace, made his first public address in America today at the Church of the Ascension on Fifth avenue. He spoke through an interpreter, his nephew.

# ABDUL BAHA COMING TO CHICAGO MEETING

Leader of Bahai Movement, Which Is Attracting Nations of the World, Is Guest in America.

## CHARITY AND PEACE SOUGHT

Universal Brotherhood of Man and the Unity of Religious Creeds Also Objects of Search.

Abdul Baha, which is not a name, but a title, signifying "servant of God," the remarkable Persian who is at the head of the Bahai movement, which has spread to all corners of the world, and who arrived in New York yesterday on his first visit to this country, will come to Chicago on April 27 to attend the international congress of the Bahai movement and Chicago adherents of the movement are making preparations for his reception. Delegates are expected from Honolulu and other parts of the globe, as well as from assemblies in various parts of the United States.

The congress will open on the evening of the arrival of Abdul Baha with a reception to the leader and visiting delegates and will continue, according to present plans for five days. On the final day the women's Bahai assembly will give a reception to the club women of Chicago in the red ballroom of the Hotel La Salle, and Abdul Baha will address them. In this connection it may be stated that he is in favor of woman suffrage, an advocate of equality for women, not in politics only, but in all things else.

Teaches Brotherhood of Men.
His movement, although it orig

www.ingramcontent.com/pod-product-compliance
Lightning Source LLC
La Vergne TN
LVHW051634080426

835511LV00016B/2337